The Supervisor's Companion

A practical guide for new
(and lightly trained) supervisors

By Jeanne Thomas Hugg

For my loving dad, George D. Thomas,
who has been my inspiration on this life journey.

Website:

www.thesupervisorscompanion.com

Email:

jeanne@thesupervisorscompanion.com

Contents

Introduction

I have met some spectacular people throughout my professional journey. Most have added richness to my life, teaching me lessons I would not have experienced if life had taken a different course. One person, Sherri, a co-founder of a scientific company, suggested that I write a book on supervision so that there would be a helpful reference for her and her staff. That's how this started.

The idea that I would ever write a book seemed a bit absurd, but I decided to ask others if such a book would be helpful. I heard a resounding, 'Yes!' every time I asked. Many people gave me topics to include and, without asking if I were going to actually write such a book, most of them said they wanted a copy when I was done. Were they kidding? They really thought I was going to do this? Now I was getting stuck. I guess my questions implied I had made a decision. Then they began asking about my progress on the project. What could I do? Clearly, untrained supervisors were hungering for practical information. Maybe it *was* time to write down some of the experiences and knowledge I had acquired along the way. So here we are.

The first supervisory job I had was at Northwestern University when I was just twenty-five years old. I was hired as an instructor and clinical supervisor for pediatric audiology post grads – my first profession. I had my Master's degree and all the requisite certifications, including two years of work experience. I felt fully prepped and ready to go. Of course, I hadn't so much as supervised a cat, much less a human, but I wasn't going to tell a soul. I was good to go.

Youth and inexperience can provide just the right amount of blurriness when it comes to estimating actual abilities. I thought I could do anything, regardless of how scared or inexperienced I was. If there was a problem (or two, or three), I'd figure it out when I got to it. This quality can be useful in a young, enthusiastic person eager for life experiences. Being willing to jump in is what helps us grow and gives us opportunities we wouldn't otherwise have. However, these qualities can have a downside.

When someone is responsible for training, motivating and leading others, unbridled enthusiasm and an overconfident ego can cause problems. As I learned then and more clearly throughout my professional life, I was sorely unprepared for supervisory responsibilities. Giving it a whirl without any training had some unpleasant consequences.

Ten years later, I transitioned into a new career in human resources. There, I obtained the required training to supervise and manage others. Life offered new experiences and, like many maturing adults, I developed a more balanced sense of myself and my capabilities. I was re-introduced to my passion – teaching. I love to teach and coach others. Over time it became clear to me how many newly promoted supervisors are sent off to their new jobs with little or no preparation. Frankly, it was obvious that there were a whole bunch of supervisors – newbies and veterans - struggling with how to effectively supervise their employees. Everyone was winging it, just like me so many years ago. And no one was telling.

It has been my pleasure to work with these supervisors, most of whom are thirsty to learn new skills and tools. Teaching groups is cost effective, and I like the interaction. Good information is shared and everyone can gain a lot in this format. Sometimes, though, the implementation suffered. When the class was over, it was often difficult to apply the new information, and management was not necessarily on the same page. Receiving individualized coaching proved to be a bit more satisfying to many of these supervisors. There is a sense of confidentiality in individual meetings. Our solutions were specific and practical. I could meet with the supervisor's manager if necessary, broker difficult situations, and actually provide customized training. We could make progress. One of my goals in writing this book is to serve you specifically – address your needs, enhance your strengths and give you a sense that you are not alone in this difficult journey. Becoming an effective supervisor is difficult. Being a supervisor is difficult. From time to time you need a companion. Let this book serve you.

The concept of supervision is pretty simple – you train new employees, you help them to do their jobs, and sometimes you handle difficult situations. It sounds easy, but it's not. If you do it well, first line supervision is likely the most difficult job in any organization. Dealing daily with the hoard of issues people have is taxing. Sometimes, it's hard to feel successful. Don't get discouraged, though, because effective supervision is rewarding in many ways.

This book is written to bring the new or untrained supervisor into the process. I use real world experiences and offer tools and ideas to help you solve everyday problems. This book is meant to be practical, not theoretical.

There is no perfect supervisor and no perfect employee. We all struggle with one pesky condition – being human. But, when work needs to get done by people in a group, someone needs to lead the effort. Everyone in the group approaches work differently, has different skill sets and responds differently to situations. Who can make that work perfectly all the time? No one, but I am hopeful that as you gain new information, you will up the odds of success. I don't want to just give you practical information. My primary intent is to encourage flexibility of thinking in the challenges of each day. I hope by the time you have finished reading this, you will have what you need to help both you and your employees be successful.

ॐ

The his-and-her and he-and-she thing ...

Writing a nonfiction book to connect with each of you can be a bit tricky at times. Are you a he or a she? Should I write he/she each time I need a pronoun other than me or they? Will using one pronoun throughout the book make it easier? I figured that doesn't make sense, so I just randomly inserted "he" and "she" as it seemed to flow in the writing. I never counted to make sure the pronoun reference was equal, but my hope is there is enough of a sense of balance for everyone to enjoy and be comfortable with the message.

Did that really happen?

The stories I tell in this book are meant to highlight a teaching point or idea. While all of the stories reflect an experience, the names of many of the people and locations have been changed. Some of the events and people are composites of several individual events or persons.

What is supervision?

My first supervisory job outside of the academic world was in a medical office. When I arrived, the place was a mess – folders were everywhere, information was mis-filed and there was food and drinks on every desk and file top. The office staff seemed perpetually unhappy and disorganized. Even more disturbing was that no one seemed to care, except for one lovely young lady who followed me around like a long lost soul. I had my work cut out for me. I was sorely unprepared for the job. Remember, I had only supervised students until this point. Up to now I thought I was pretty good at supervision. It turns out that students will do what you tell them to do because that's what students *need* to do to get a decent grade and graduate. I was about to learn that the real world was very different.

At first I figured that if I just cleaned up the place, the staff would appreciate my efforts and pitch in to keep it that way. I worked tirelessly over a long week end and proudly came to work on Tuesday with not so much as a howdy-do. Then I thought, 'Well, I'll implement some efficient work flow systems and that should help.' I explained everything thoroughly but I had a hard time figuring out why only a few of the staff would follow the systems as I had explained. I was working so hard and trying to set a good example, which I thought would get the staff to rally around me and make this the best

1

office, but the staff showed little appreciation for my efforts. How could I improve morale, enthusiasm, work effort and productivity? How could I succeed at this most difficult job? I had a lot to learn and a long way to go.

One of the things I learned early in my new career was that people's view of what a supervisor is, and does, varies greatly. Before I started to write this book, I decided to get a sense of what people in various work environments and at various employee levels think supervision is. Sometimes, I would get a long lecture on the evils of supervision and how some supervisors make work-life miserable. Sometimes, I heard high praise for a supervisor who got it right. The responses were as varied as the people I asked.

Here are some excerpts from my interviews to give you a sense of how differently people see this kind of work:

- ✧ *Supervision is the front line coordination of every thing.* [manager in medical testing company]

- ✧ *I think of supervision as someone who manages over the employees to make sure the job is done correctly. Everything needs to be done well.* [server in a chain restaurant]

- ✧ *The supervisor is the boss. I do what he says.* [grocery store clerk]

- ✧ *Most of the supervisors I've had have made my life miserable, so you don't really want to know what I think.* [help desk technician]

⤙ *It's oversight of the employees so that all reach the common goal.* [executive at a bank]

⤙ *Being a supervisor is like being someone's mom. You've got to make sure they get their work done, pick up after them when they don't, and listen to them complain a lot. I don't much like this job. [office manager in a legal firm]*

We supervise our staff differently because we see the job differently. How we view the job affects how we handle the job. If we view the job negatively, we will likely approach our work negatively. To the contrary, when we see opportunity and success, we will approach our efforts with that attitude. Sometimes we *do* need to broaden or enlighten our perspective. When this happens we can become more receptive to learning the tools and methods of a successful supervisor.

Supervisors, managers, executives and staff agreed that there is a huge gap (if not an abyss) when going from a staffer to being a new supervisor. Every supervisor with whom I spoke was grateful for or hoped for some basic training. I knew there was a need for this book.

What is an effective supervisor?

One way to define a supervisor is as an individual who gets employees to cooperate in meeting organizational goals within set time and cost restraints. But a supervisor needs to be more than that. My definition of a supervisor includes helping each employee satisfy professional needs and objectives.

Supervisors get things done through people and in turn help employees succeed at their jobs.

∾

Managers as supervisors

In most organizations, managers have supervisory responsibilities. However, managers usually have expanded work efforts, such as directing the activities of more than one work group and managing the recruitment, staffing and budgets of those groups. Often managers will have supervisors of various units report the progress and work issues directly to them.

In a company with the traditional organizational structure, the manager will supervise the supervisors. The supervisor is directly responsible for the implementation of the work through the general staff in one unit. While not every company will have such a structure, it is clear that managers need to have supervisory skills in order to make sure the work effort is successfully accomplished.

It is often assumed, sometimes wrongly, that managers received supervisory training when they got their first promotion to supervisor. It is also assumed quite often, and again sometimes wrongly, that these managers will be skilled in the area of supervision. It is assumed that they will understand what motivates employees, how to manage deficient performance, delegate and run effective meetings. Anyone who is reading this book knows that may not be the case. When you are finished reading *The Supervisor's Companion*, share it. This book is written for the benefit of every employee.

The supervisor helps employees get the job done.

Communication

That which sets us apart from the animal kingdom
doesn't necessarily elevate us.

∽

When it comes to supervising, communication is the
biggie. We'll be reviewing the many aspects of communication. Most of us have so little understanding of
how to effectively communicate our thoughts, feelings
or information that I am stunned the system works
at all. Sadly, we also are quite limited in understanding how our communication affects others. Have you
ever walked away from what you thought was a positive conversation with someone only to learn later that
your comments were very upsetting? We can be clueless
about how what we say is perceived.

As a species, we've neglected to develop this skill to its
greatest potential. We take a good shot at this as children, learning vocabulary and grammar. Once we get
the vocabulary and grammar established, first verbally
and then in written form, we think we are good to go.
But those elements are the least important factors to
become an effective communicator.

The consequences of not developing our communication skills past the basics are overwhelming. Deficient

communication skills can lead to misunderstandings, arguments, sorrow and sometimes even violence. Sometimes this is because of ignorance or naïve thinking, either thoughtless or deliberate. Sometimes, we just don't care. That's not an option as a supervisor.

I am heartened by my clients' desires to be good supervisors – their desires to have a positive influence on employees' professional lives. At the same time, I am confounded by the knowledge gap many of my clients have when it comes to understanding how their communication is really affecting people. Many of my clients struggle with how to move from the *desire* to be an effective supervisor to the *implementation* of that process.

Our communication skills and needs are so intimately intertwined with our emotional skills and needs that it's difficult to separate them. Supervisors are just like everyone else and chances are they always have a couple of personal issues going on. These battles can decrease communicative sensitivity, but there are some basic tools we can apply, regardless of our personal issues. This will improve professional communication.

The communication gap

Poor communication is the top complaint I have heard from staffers in every company where I have worked. The results from numerous employee satisfaction surveys I have conducted over the years indicate that 80 percent (or more) of the participating employees complain about their supervisor's poor communication. A review of the last three employee satisfaction surveys I conducted indicated that communication complaints are twice as frequent as compared with any other topic – even compensation.

Some complaints include:

> *My supervisor only speaks with me when I do something wrong.*

> *My supervisor mostly emails me when she has something to say.*

> *My supervisor communicates with me only during my annual performance review.*

> *I'm never sure what my supervisor wants.*

Do any of these complaints ring true for you?

When I report the results of my surveys to management, or even to the staff at large, most react with alarm at this information and ask who could be so callous. I shake my head as I watch this scenario over and over again. Some of these comments apply to the very managers or supervisors most appalled by this information.

Some employees would rather not talk to the supervisor very often. That view may change when the supervisor discusses performance issues during the annual review meeting, as required. Suddenly everything goes awry. This doesn't mean that supervisors need to chit-chat or talk a lot, or even often, to employees. However, they do owe their employees a sense of how things are going before the stressful reviews take place.

Take a break from reading...

Look around.

What do you think your employees would say to me in a survey?

When did you last talk to your junior employee about what he is looking for long term?

Have you offered any training or coaching lately?

Have you been too busy?

Be honest with yourself and take account of how things are going in your department.

What are the primary communication components?

How often have you heard that laugh that just doesn't seem so happy? Have you seen those folded arms and bored look while you were trying to convince someone to implement that spiffy new idea of yours? Have you ever completely tuned someone out, but know exactly when it's your turn to speak? Subtle visual clues are very powerful. These situations confirm that communication is more than just words.

Albert Mehrabian, Ph.D., author of *Silent Messages*, formulated the 7%-38%-55% rule that describes the three elements in any face-to-face communication – verbal, tonal and body language. His studies indicate that only seven percent of our communication is via words – just seven percent. So much for that fancy vocabulary.

While his research is specifically applicable to the communication of attitudes and feelings, I'd like to apply this formula more broadly for the sake of simplicity and perspective in this book. For example, while the percentage of influence may be debatable, there is a basic recognition that body language has a huge impact on communication. So if we are willing to accept the relative impact of verbal, tonal and body movement that Mehrabian proposes, we can accept that words are not as influential to communication as we might think. I am moving forward with this premise as we seek to increase our effective use of various communication tools.

Let's add another element to communication – listening. Many of us aren't very good listeners. We tend to be thinking about our reply, or maybe something totally unrelated, while someone is talking. When it's time to reply, we are utterly unprepared. Maybe we were so busy planning our reply that we missed a lot of what the speaker was saying. When active listening skills aren't developed, we fail to be strong communicators. Add this to the top of your 'to do' list.

Body language

Body language communicates most of the message.

We are intuitively aware of the value of body language when communicating a message. We know, for example, that a certain glance will stop the talkative person one row behind us at the movies. Who hasn't observed the 'knowing look' between a couple when the mother-in-law starts reminding them it's time to make her some grandbabies. A simple smile can welcome the most reluctant communicator and maybe prompt a friendship to boot. These are obvious examples of non-verbal communication. Sometimes, we just communicate through body language because it's easier or will keep a perceived threat at bay.

You don't need to be a body language expert to know the basics. Facial expressions, such as a smile or frown, are clear. Hands open versus closed in a fist suggest a relaxed listener versus a tense listener. There are subtleties, too. Most people think that someone will be less responsive if their arms are crossed than if their arms are open. However, look at the overall picture. Sometimes people can relax and focus with crossed arms. They're just more comfortable that way. Look at how they're sitting – facing you or slightly turned away. Is it cold in the room and maybe crossed arms are keeping them warm? Are they attentive, looking directly at you with a neutral or warm expression? The crossed arms might not be relevant here. People who are sensitive to body language pick up on cues easily. Others don't. As a supervisor, observing body language and being aware of your own is an essential skill to develop.

Remember, body language accounts for a large portion of the communication you will have with your staff.

If you are busy looking into a computer monitor while someone is talking, you may be missing more than half of the message. Perhaps more importantly, over half of the message you are sending is that you aren't really paying attention or don't care.

Maybe you're not sure if this is an issue for you, so have trusted friends clue you in. Watch the expression of someone you are talking to. Did it change before you spoke? Is your body language consistent with your verbal message? This self-awareness will ensure that you are sending a message consistent with the words you speak and the message you intend.

Body language is the first welcome sign.

Think about how you welcome visitors to your work-space. A smile will do more to relax and welcome a visitor than any other message. The rule of thumb is to look up and acknowledge your visitor – use that smile. If you are busy, say that. If more than a couple of minutes are necessary and you don't have that time, give a specific time frame – like, "In an hour," or, "At 3:00" is even better. Unless it's something urgent, your visitor now knows that there is a timeslot set aside and that you do value the meeting.

However, if you do have time when someone stops by, make sure your full, face-forward attention is given. Encourage visitors to sit if there's a chair. Show that you are prepared to listen. Lean forward on your desk, or open your arms and sit back to show you are ready to receive concerns or questions. These suggestions may seem quite fundamental. But I know that a few of you are saying, "Really, I need to do that?" Yes, these basics will get you off to a good start. It won't carry you for long, but it's a start.

Are you hiding behind body language?

Surprisingly, one of the problems with body language is that we can hide behind it – just like a reluctant teenager when getting grilled by parents. Teens like the shrug. Most of us know that it's easier to send a negative message with subtle body language. When a child is misbehaving in public, isn't it easier to just use that stern facial expression rather than verbally calling attention to the situation? The "Mom face" usually works pretty well.

The problem with a supervisor using body language as a primary communication method is that your employee deserves a more complete message. Forcing your employee to interpret messages because *you* are more comfortable with delivering nonverbal cues will not always turn out well.

Unless we're talking about a big smile right after something good happens, a subordinate will rarely interpret vague or incomplete messages positively. Incomplete or unclear messages are confusing and confusion is uncomfortable. At such times we may ask other employees what they think happened. This further dilutes and confuses the message. It's not likely the person you consulted for clarification of this second-hand information is going to make anything better. The "consultant" may actually add to the confusion, further pointing us in a negative direction. We're vulnerable and unsure.

One of my directors was very uncomfortable in individual meetings and would avoid one-on-one communication whenever possible. It was a new job, and I thought it was important that we meet regularly to build a professional relationship and plan the development of a new human resource department. I didn't know what my new director thought about meetings. He just nodded in agreement when I requested these meetings shortly after my arrival. I should have paid better attention to that nod.

When I showed up for my first meeting, Jim had his head buried in a computer monitor. I waited a respectable moment or two and then said, "Jim, are you ready to meet?" Another nod. Uh oh. So, I sat down and, after a bit of preamble, gave him my initial proposal for developing the human resource department. I have to admit I could sense Jim wasn't engaged but, against my better instincts, I forged on. Finally, he took the document, scanned it briefly and then tossed it over his head to presumably land on his desk. He was a poor shot and the proposal landed in the trash can. This was not a good start.

When a relationship begins like this, it isn't likely to improve. Unfortunately, I have learned that uncomfortable experiences, like mine, are more common than you might think. If you want to make the relationship work, you will need to put in a great deal of effort – ego aside and plod on.

I'm not saying that strong body language isn't a good idea with some employees, or even from time to time when an intense workload may excuse a strong, "Not now," message. However, as a general form of communication, body language alone just doesn't cut it. It will likely diminish the odds of any kind of positive relationship with your employee. You need to speak, too.

Tone of voice

I wasn't surprised that tone of voice is such a large part of communication. The memory of my teenage daughter saying, "*Fine*" when I asked her to do something flooded my mind. If you've had a teenage daughter you know that "fine" right? You know what it means and you know she's not a happy camper. Trouble is brewing. There are plenty of jokes about the wife who, in response to her husband's query about whether she is ok about something, replies, "*Fine,*" when she really isn't. Daggers could emanate from that kind of "fine." The word fine isn't so fine all the time.

There is no place in the work environment for sarcasm or a curt response. Loud speech or monotone replies all convey negative emotions that inflame negative feelings and hamper communication. If you are irritated with someone, they get the message through sarcasm. But do they really modify their behavior or work efforts if you just send strong negative signals through your tone?

Voice tone is probably easier to control than body language, which can be more subtle and reflect truer emotions. Tone is really something we deliberately add to communication. The listener receives messages much better with a neutral tone. That's an essential skill for supervisors to develop.

Without speaking a word, you know when your employee wants to talk to you.

🦶 What does your **body language** convey?

> ➤ Are you ready to listen?

> ➤ Are you looking at the employee?

> ➤ Are you glancing at your computer monitor?

> ➤ Are you frowning?

> ➤ Where is that smile?

> ➤ Tapping your toes?

> ➤ Throwing stuff (seriously)?

🦶 What does your **tone of voice** convey?

> ➤ Are you willing to listen?

> ➤ Do you sound angry?

> ➤ Is there sarcasm when you say, "What do you want"?

> ➤ Are your emotions under control?

> ➤ Do you sound shrill?

> ➤ Is there aggression in your voice?

NOTES:

The art of listening

True or false: While someone is talking to me, I am often preparing my reply.

Check one:

☐ True

☐ False

Ok, now let's see how honest you were with yourself. Start a conversation with someone about a topic you're interested in. Then, pay attention to your behavior. Are you thinking ahead? Are you twitching in excitement, as you think about what you will say? Are you nodding a lot as an indication that you are finished listening? At the slightest pause, do you interrupt and share your own wonderful thoughts? When the conversation has come to an end, can you really tell someone what the other person said?

Now, take the re-test:

True or false: While someone is talking to me, I am often preparing my reply.

Check one:

☐ True

☐ False

If you were honest with yourself, you probably replied "true" the second time. I can certainly reply "true." I love to talk. Listening is such a bother. Listening takes effort and, besides, I have so much left to say. Frankly, I just like to share what I think. You too?

Poor listening skills are a common affliction for many of us. Effective listening becomes even more trying when there are emotions involved – when one or both communicators have a stake in the outcome. When listening decreases, misunderstandings increase. We might think we're communicating, but, for many of us, **the goal is to convince our listener rather than understand his message.** Sharing thoughts becomes a one way street. This is a problem in general, and it becomes a problem when the new supervisor does not develop active listening skills. Before we discuss the speaking part of verbal communication, let's focus on the listening part.

Remember going on that first date and wondering what to talk about? How about that job interview? What questions will you ask when it's your turn? Have you worried about going to that work gathering? Do you want to know how to resolve these anxieties? Simple – first, learn to listen. Well, the learning part of that phrase isn't so simple.

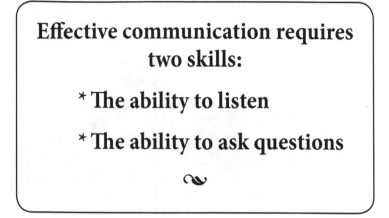

Effective communication requires
two skills:

* The ability to listen

* The ability to ask questions

Are you a 'lazy' listener?

Many of us are lazy listeners. There are many reasons why we're lazy, including cultural ones. Ever watched those political pundits on TV? Two pundits sit facing the host, one in favor of the topic and one against. A well-crafted question is posed – then you see it. "My opinion is blah, blah, blah." "He's wrong because my opinion is blah, blah, blah." The "blah, blah, blahs" are sound-bites that have nothing to do with the question or with the first pundit's reply. Soon yelling ensues. Good TV, perhaps, but not one shred of listening. Just telling and yelling. Is this the way communication is supposed to be? Imagine children hearing this kind of behavior. This is cultural learning at work. We are learning to speak without listening.

However, we can't blame TV or cultural influences for our own lazy listening. We are pretty good at lazy listening all by ourselves. Most of us would much rather share our thoughts or correct other people's thoughts than listen.

During my initial meetings with a new client, I assess the active, established listening skills. After I feel comfortable and connected with my client, I'll raise a topic of conversation that both of us are interested in. It usually involves some aspect of work such as, "What about that new department, eh?" or, "I see you have Friday Breakfast Club." I'll describe my thoughts about the topic. I try to keep it pretty neutral, but will insert something that should raise an opinion. Of course, and not surprisingly, my client's opinions are expressed quickly.

Before I leave the session, I ask what my client understood about my views on the topic. Not surprisingly, few clients remember much. To assess communication skill improvement, I repeat this exercise at the end of each session. If there's no improvement, I know we haven't made much progress in developing communication skills. Maybe my opinions aren't that interesting, but cut me some slack here and focus on the point, ok? Supervisors have to learn to actually hear the perspective of the staff whether they like the perspective or not.

Learning to listen is difficult. I was raised in a family where asking questions was considered "nosey." It was a definite no-no. My family is more geared to sharing facts rather than personal information or feelings. I entered the real world thinking that, to make conversation with someone, I just had to know lots of facts or have lots of ideas. Fortunately I met Rick, who would become my husband. Rick's family had a very different way of communicating than mine did. I was absolutely enchanted watching my husband's mother ask probing, though not threatening, questions. Everyone was engaged and animated as they shared. My grandmother was someone who gave me affection and cookies, but I don't remember her asking what I thought about something. I was on full alert watching my new soon-to-be family share real thoughts and feelings with each other.

I soon brought Rick to a party to meet my work friends. The next day, everyone told me what an interesting person Rick was. Really? The sensitive nature of his work, which he couldn't discuss, and the fact that he's pretty private about his personal life made me wonder what was so interesting. Not that I didn't think he was interesting, but describing Rick as "one of the most interesting people" seemed over the top. Maybe he just picked good conversation topics. Well, as it turns out, Rick and his family are master listeners. He seemed more interesting to others because he was interested in what they were saying. Wow, what a fascinating concept! I've spent 36 years of marriage trying to learn this skill, and it isn't easy. But if you can develop this skill, it pays off big time. **Active listening will be your most effective supervisory tool.**

How to be an active listener

Becoming an active listener requires approaching a situation with an open and curious mind.

This is tough, especially for a supervisor who wants to be sure everything "goes right" – or more specifically, "goes the way I want it to." You can't listen well if you are only prepared to tell.

- Telling isn't listening.

- There is no open mind in telling.

- There is no listening in telling.

If you spend most of your time telling your employees what to do and how to do things, you aren't listening and learning from your employees. Think about that.

I remember one of my first clients, Roger, who was a classic micromanager. Micromanagers are generally poor listeners. I like to role play with my clients if

27

they are agreeable. We set up a situation where Roger was struggling with managing an employee who was frequently late to work. I played the employee, Susan. Roger's goal was to engage in dialogue so he could determine if there were extenuating circumstances to explain Susan's chronic tardiness. We had discussed active listening and I thought I had prepared Roger well for the exercises. After the preliminaries he just sat there, finally admitting, "I don't know what to ask." Well, try starting with the obvious. Why are you late? He did that and, as Susan, I said that I just had trouble getting started in the morning. Roger got that glassy eyed look and then just launched into telling me why I had to be on time, what it was doing to the morale in the group, etc. On and on he went and slowly "Susan" shut down.

Roger needed to learn the value of the open question. An open question indicates interest on a broad level. It also indicates that you are seeking information and not the "right answer." If Roger had asked an open question, such as, "Can you expand on that?" he would have had a more productive conversation – and an engaged employee. By asking an open question, Roger would project a genuine desire to help Susan. Then he would have discovered that, while employed full time, Susan was also trying to care for her ill husband. Further inquiry with open questions and active listening would have alerted Roger that Susan's problem was short term. A slight, temporary modification to her schedule could help Susan and not brand her as a deficient employee. True, she could have come to Roger and asked for that, but she was shy and somewhat fearful of Roger's response.

Employees need to know that their supervisor is prepared to listen. This is the supervisor's job. Had Roger handled this differently, when Susan first started coming in late, the conversations would not have been so uncomfortable and his perception of Susan would have been more positive. Changes could have been made for an overall win-win. Equally important is that Susan would have seen that she had a compassionate supervisor, who cares about his employees, and not just someone who's a timekeeper. Big brownie points there for Roger!

Becoming an active listener requires focusing on another person during a conversation.

We have very busy brains. We're easily distracted and in this hectic world it's difficult to focus on someone else. This happens frequently in the supervisor's day. Since technology keeps us so connected, we value multitasking. However, when an employee has an issue or concern, your full focus is far more valuable. That can be difficult, but this is a skill you need to practice and perfect if you want to succeed as a supervisor.

To help with this, when an employee needs to discuss something with you that requires 100% attention, set a meeting time and place with minimal distractions. Mute the phone, close the door and look directly at your employee. That's a good start.

Becoming an active listener means asking open-ended questions.

This is the tricky part about active listening, because most of us don't know how to ask a good question. Here's one:

How can I help you?

This is probably the best question a supervisor can ask. It probably does more for employee relations and problem solving than any other question you could come up with.

Remember that one. It works in almost every situation.

How can I help you?

I had another client, Norma, who worked for the public school system. Repeatedly, she was privy to conversations between a principal and a struggling teacher. Time and again, the principal would list all of the teacher's deficiencies and then give her instructions on improving. Not once did the principal ask why the teacher was having trouble, what she needed to perform her job more effectively, or if there was any training the teacher felt would be helpful. Not one open-ended question.

Not once did Norma hear this principal, someone committed to learning and nurturing young children, ask, *"How can I help you?"*

Open-ended questions give employees opportunities to say what he or she thinks or needs. For example, asking the teacher how she thinks she is doing with the student assessment process, rather than telling her that she is doing it wrong, will yield a very different response.

Open-ended questions need to be just that – open for comment.

By now this is pretty obvious. The best communicators listen more and say less.

Silence is golden.

You'll be amazed at the information available if you allow your employee plenty of time to speak. We get very uncomfortable with dead air. If a supervisor says to an employee, "So, why do you think you're having trouble with that technique?" how long will the supervisor wait for the reply? Probably not long – maybe only seconds – before the need to fill in the silence kicks in. You need to wait. Just wait. Silence, quiet, "oh-my-gosh-please-answer..." Wait. If you wait for the reply, you will likely receive the information you need. You also demonstrate that you're interested in your employee's perspective and your employee feels heard. Big bonus points for you, the supervisor.

* Becoming an active listener requires that you approach an interaction with *an open and curious mind*

* Becoming an active listener requires *focusing on the other person* during a conversation

* Becoming an active listener means *asking open-ended questions*

* Becoming an active listener means *saying less*

∾

The verbal component of communication

Making words from thoughts is difficult. We are unsure of our vocabulary and grammar and that makes us uncomfortable. "I don't speak well. I wish I could say it like you do," are comments I hear frequently from my clients. Words come easily to me. I love to talk. I like to try and persuade people using language. But I have learned that fancy phrasing, quick retorts or advanced vocabulary aren't more influential or helpful to the listener than simple vocabulary and phrasing – provided the basic information is there. You don't need a big vocabulary for that. It has been my experience that in order to improve the clarity of your communication, it's best to use simple words and short phrases. Fancy vocabulary words can be off-putting. Often, that's what the speaker intends. As a supervisor, that's the last thing you want.

The verbally talented man is not better understood than the simply spoken man. If your listener understands what you want to convey, you have succeeded.

Verbal Communication Rule #1: At least say hello

Let's start with the basics –just say, "Hi." One of my easiest clients, Greta, began our first session seeking help with a "difficult" employee. Greta was a delightful person. She was warm and friendly, beloved by all. She had a loyal staff who worked hard for her. However, she couldn't seem to reach one employee. Will was an older gentleman and in a second career after serving in the Marines Corps where he retired as a Master Sergeant.

He had worked in quality control at this company for six years and had a reputation of resisting training and not being a team player. Management had moved Will from department to department in an attempt to find a supervisor who could manage him. Greta was his newest supervisor.

After hearing her concerns, I asked Greta if she had met with Will. She admitted that she hadn't and that she was uncomfortable arranging such a meeting. Will intimidated her.

"He always seems grumpy, not friendly at all," she said. "He won't even acknowledge me to say good morning. He stays to himself and, really, no one wants to talk to him. I am very uncomfortable trying to meet with him."

I was wondering what was so scary about this man. "Has he verbally or physically hurt you or someone else? Does he seem aggressive in some way? Look scary to you? What is it that intimidates you about him?"

"He just isn't friendly. I don't like approaching someone who acts like he doesn't like me."

"Have you even said 'hello' to him?" I asked.

"No".

Somewhat astounded, I affirmed "Nothing? No acknowledgement of him just because he seems unfriendly?"

"No, I haven't met with him" she replied sheepishly.

"Assignment one – say hello, make eye contact and smile warmly when you greet him. There is nothing further you need to do. I'll see you in a week." Greta seemed a little disappointed that I hadn't come up with some miracle cure for this "difficult" employee, but she said that she would do as I instructed.

When I met with Greta the following week, she could hardly contain herself. Will had responded well to the first greeting. It was just a responsive nod, but it encouraged Greta. Each day she would greet Will and over the course of the week their interaction grew. By Friday, they were spending some time each morning chatting about the upcoming day and the work load ahead. Will began to share some information about his personal life – a little about his family and their move to the area.

Greta was shocked. She had never imagined that Will would respond to her, much less chat about various topics. When I met with her again, she was embarrassed to admit that her preconceived ideas about Will had prevented her from even being friendly. I prompted Greta to arrange a meeting with Will where training needs, professional development and goals would be discussed. Within three weeks, Will and Greta had a productive and interactive working relationship. His prior supervisors were happy to see that Will had "finally improved."

Had Will "finally improved" – or did something else happen?

Verbal Communication Rule # 2: The more you listen the better you'll speak

This topic has been covered pretty well earlier in the book, but it bears mentioning again. If you want to improve your communication skills, listening and verbal communication must work together. Knowing what to say mostly depends on what you hear. Remember that you can't respond well if you don't know what the speaker said and meant.

Verbal Communication Rule #3: Avoid emotional trigger words or phrases

My good friend, Kathy, called me one day to ask advice about an interaction she had with her supervisor. Kathy has always prided herself on being a productive employee. She repeatedly had excellent performance reviews and was well regarded by her fellow employees. On the day of her call, however, she was quite upset because her supervisor began expressing concerns about trust.

By her own admission, Kathy had not kept her supervisor up to date on the progress of a training program she was developing. Her supervisor, Elise, was understandably concerned. Kathy apologized and said she'd improve in this area when suddenly Elise said, "I'm not sure I can trust you again, Kathy." A conversation directed simply toward performance suddenly struck deeply at Kathy's character.

The next day Elise realized her mistake and told Kathy that she had gone too far. Kathy and Elise were able to move forward without damaging their relationship.

Trigger words or phrases elicit strong emotions. That's their intention. They are powerful. If they send a negative connotation they hurt. They are vague and usually strike at our character. For example, "I'm not sure I can trust you again," implies that the listener has not been honest and that she may not be honest in general. When someone has made an unintended mistake, this is way too strong and not applicable to the situation. Disrespect creeps in when someone uses these trigger words. The negative effect is immediate and deep. We are hurt to the core. It takes a strong character to apologize for this error and gracious forgiveness to accept the apology.

Most of us know these trigger words or phrases because at some point we have been on the receiving end. It just happens in life. No one is perfect and we will hurt others from time to time. However, as a supervisor, you have to work very hard to avoid this. It's difficult to undo the damage.

The table on the next page contains a sampling of negative trigger words and phrases alongside alternative phrases. Using phrases like or similar to the alternatives will more likely engage the employee and encourage productive conversation. I left two cells blank for your use. Try adding some trigger phrases and possible alternatives.

word/phrase	Suggested alternative phrasing
I can't trust you again.	I need to be able to depend on you to do this. Can you tell me why you're …?
You don't seem to care.	To do your work well, it must be important to you. Can you give me a sense of how you view your work? Let's talk about what I am observing.
You are lazy.	To perform satisfactorily, you will need to complete your work on time. Can you tell me why you are having difficulty finishing on time?
Why can't you learn this stuff?	Do you understand what needs to be done?
How many times do I need to help you?	How can I help you better understand this task? Can you tell me what might help you work independently?
What's wrong with you?	You seem to be having some difficulty. Let's talk about it.
You have an attitude.	You seem upset. I notice that you are arguing with other people on the team. I am concerned about this. Let's talk about it.
I am disappointed in you.	Your performance isn't improving as much as it needs to. Let's spend some time working on this

To increase the likelihood that your listener "hears" what you say:

- 🐚 Only discuss performance or behavior observations that concern you.

- 🐚 Stick with the facts.

- 🐚 Stay far away from generalities and comments that speak to a person's character.

- 🐚 Avoid trigger words.

NOTES:

The Role of Technology

The good, the bad and the useful

I have bit of a beef with technology when it comes to communication. Technology for information exchange is a good thing. Technology to exchange thoughts and feelings at work – not so much.

Remember when I told you about the high value of body language and tone of voice in communication? Let's think about the printed or digital words hanging there for ages without any sense of body language or voice context. We're depending on a small percentage of our communication tools – just the words – that we have at our disposal to make our message clear. When those words are conveyed quickly through email or text exchange with no other contextual clues, the odds for success are not very good, particularly for a supervisor.

"Thanks a lot" without the addition of body language or tone of voice can be interpreted in different ways. For example, in the world of face to face human inter-action, "Thanks a lot," from a disgruntled customer in a retail store sounds and looks very different from the "Thanks a lot," your friend says after you help paint her living room. The words are the same, but the message that is conveyed will be different because of your body language and tone of voice. You just can't do that in an email or text.

 Some of you might be thinking, "Well, we have **bolding** and <u>underlining</u> for emphasis and CAPITAL LETTER-ING for screaming." And then there are the valuable emoticons for *really* conveying how we feel. I'm pretty sure most of you know that using emoticons is gener-ally not acceptable in professional writing – just a little reminder.

I've received many email stories from employees and clients over the years. Maybe you've been the recipient of similar emails.

- *My supervisor sends the email message on the subject line only. I get these emails only when he is upset with me or my performance.*

- *My supervisor never responds to my emails.*

- *My supervisor will write on and on about what I didn't do well. He won't meet with me and won't fol-low up.*

- *My supervisor forwards my performance appraisal as an email attachment with no comments.*

- *I call my supervisor the Email Nag because every day I get an email with reminders of what needs to be done. She has some kind of code, which I am not sure how to break, but she uses red for some tasks, bold for others, and I'm guessing that the red and bold with caps is really important. It's not like she meets with me about this stuff. I just get the emails.*

↝ *When I asked my supervisor to approve time off, the reply simply said "NO." Did he really need to send an email scream for that request?*

↝ *My manager copies all managers up through the president on her emails to me. She does a "reply all" to every follow up email, no matter how trivial.*

Technology is terrific for sending a quick reminder of a meeting or deadline and it's useful for transmitting work documents and plans. Technology can organize information and preserve trees by saving our words in ether-land or on a hard drive. Technology can save time and make connection immediate. Most of us are connected 24/7 now. Unfortunately, technology can't resolve human conflict or convey genuine emotion. You can't manage human beings when you rely mostly on technology for communication. Email and texting is indispensible in the business world today. But, like other things in life, too much of a good thing can be – well, not so good.

Technology as a tool for documenting performance

What about using email to document performance deficiencies? This seems to makes sense, but I am not a strong advocate for using email in this fashion. Email **can provide documentation that you asked an employee to complete a task.** It **can even validate that you told the employee about deficiencies** in performing that task. What email exchanges **cannot provide is dialogue with the employee.** Email does not offer an interactive opportunity to learn about the employee's perspective or about possible extenuating circumstances. It won't show a conversation exploring the lack of training in the area or any misunderstandings on your part. Emails meant to document poor performance do not usually provide the full story and, in the end, might even make the supervisor look petty and inadequate.

I am not saying that you shouldn't keep emails as a part of the poor performance employee documentation. Email documentation can augment performance management meetings, but should not be used in their stead. You will need to give your employee plenty of time to discuss any deficiencies and improvement plans with you. Keep notes of these meetings. Keep information that demonstrates your employees have received the necessary training to improve. Later, you might be required to show that you used a <u>variety of tools</u> to help your employee succeed. Email alone will not be enough.

Technology is for sharing information, not emotions

Welcome to Planet Jibibbi

Let me tell you about Planet Jibibbi –somewhere far, far away. Earthlings want to go to Planet Jibibbi and hope to be selected for a visit, where they will learn a new culture and new skills. Jibibbi is a beautiful place to visit. The environment is stimulating and exciting. Earthlings who are selected to go to Jibibbi even get money for going there.

Things are different at Planet Jibibbi. First of all, words are read backwards and right to left, like this: Sdrawkcab. It can take a while to learn how to read Jibibbi, but new visitors are very motivated to learn since they will get more money if they excel here. Lots of Earthlings work hard to learn this skill.

Jibibbians greet each other by extending their legs straight up and giving a tap-tap-tap on the ball of the foot. Admittedly, it looks a little strange, but it is the best greeting one can master. It's worth practicing because it's important to have a warm greeting for your new Jibibbian friends.

Jibibbians tell time by the nibit, rather than by the hour. There are 23.4 nibits per gramel, so if you want to get things done in a timely fashion, you need to know how many nibits are needed to arrive at the proper gramel.

To have a good visit at Planet Jibibbi, Earthlings who are selected need to be well prepared and willing to practice their new skills and cultural traditions to fit in. Almost every adult Earthling is excited to go to Jibibbi and wants to be a good guest.

Congratulations – you've just been selected to visit Planet Jibibbi. There are two continents on this planet and you will be living on one of them. Continent Right Way has a leader who is called Jibibbian Host I-Got-Your-Back. Continent Wrong Way has a leader who is called Jibibbian Host Not-So-Much.

Despite all the wonderful aspects of Planet Jibibbi has to offer, nothing here is easy or intuitive to outsiders – and you are no exception. You don't speak the language, and you don't really know the culture. You are highly dependent upon your new hosts to help you fit in.

What would really happen if you got selected to Continent Right Way on this new planet? Host I-Got-Your-Back would greet you and spend time with you. He would make you feel welcomed by showing you around and teaching you how to bump-feet-to-greet so the Jibibbians would know you were happy to meet them. Your host would introduce you to the Jibibbians you'd be spending time with. Your new home would be set up and, your training would begin immediately.

If the new skills and cultural aspects of your job were easy for you to learn, you would be praised. If you struggled, your host would help you learn and succeed. Your host would visit you from time to time during your stay to be sure you were getting the most out of your experiences. When you succeed, your host would let you know. If you just couldn't cut it, he would help you find other accommodations where there might be a better fit even if it was back at Earth. Nice, eh?

But what if you got assigned to Continent Wrong Way? Things would go quite differently. Your Host Not-So-Much would be MIA when you arrive. You'd wander aimlessly looking for someone to help you. Fortunately, Jibibbi Friend Rokko, who you greet with a handshake, offers assistance and helps you scrounge up a place to stay. Later, Rokko tells others that you are pretty ignorant and don't even know how to greet such a good Jibibbian.

You're not sure what you need to do, where or when you need to do it. You're confused and it would show. You're smart, though, so in time you catch on a bit and it feel like you're doing your best. Sadly, the concept of nibits has totally escaped you and you are branded a late-arriving-Earthling who keeps Jibibbians waiting. Host Not-So-Much steps in and tells you that you need to join the groups at 15.6 nibits and no later. Since it takes several gramels to go from place to place, and you don't know how to figure the nibits from the gramels, you're still late every day. Host Not-So-Much becomes quite upset with you. "Off you go", he says, handing you a box of your sparse work items. Not so much fun at Planet Jibibbi. You worked hard and thought you were mostly doing pretty well, so you think someone should pay for your return trip home. You'll speak to an attorney about that back at Planet Earth.

When a new employee – especially those new to the job market – arrives at his first day of work, the environment can seem as distant and confusing as Planet Jibibbi. The corporate culture, the work rules, the company anachronisms and verbal shortcuts, and the sense of isolation as the other employees socialize with their work friends can be confusing and even overwhelming at times. Employees need a 'host' or, as it works out on Planet Earth – a supervisor -- to guide them through these experiences and help them become their best work selves. What kind of host will you be?

Performance Management

Performance management is the whole enchilada. It encompasses an employee's daily performance, long- and short-term professional goals and career aspirations, and it corrects performance deficiencies when necessary. **Employee work performance management is the regular communication of expectations followed by regular feedback about how the employee is doing and how you can help.** If performance meets or exceeds expectations and your employee is satisfied with his work challenges, all is well. If his performance is not meeting expectations, you need to tell him – right away.

Most employees are solid performers. We rely on them and don't give management of good performers much thought. We tend to give negative performance and behavior much more attention. Maybe you have fifteen employees and a unit functioning like clockwork. One guy messes up and that is where you set your laser focus.

The problem for most of us is that we are uncomfortable with conflict and tension. Sometimes it feels easier to ignore the conflict. Maybe it will get better? However, every time you ignore poor performance or behavior, you're making a mistake – a very big one. Problems that are ignored or pushed aside grow and become more difficult to resolve – they don't disappear.

The communication process of performance management

By now, it's no surprise to learn that effective communication skills are the foundation for successful performance management. Let's review some basic steps in communication that can increase the chances of success for you and your employee.

Praise in public and correct in private

Except in extreme emergencies, there are no exceptions to this rule. Everyone needs recognition for their efforts. Sometimes the best kind of recognition is a public, "Thanks, good job." A private and quiet, "Thank you," is better at other times.

Criticism in public is never good. If you embarrass your employee in public, two things happen. Your other employees see you as an ogre and they are likely to be sympathetic to the poor employee you are scolding. We put ourselves in other people's shoes when we see someone being embarrassed in public. You want your employees to be comfortable in their *own* shoes.

* Praise in public
* Correct in private

Address your concerns as soon as possible.

Take the first possible opportunity to discuss a problem with an employee. Right now is better than an hour from now unless you need a little time to gather your thoughts and plan your questions and comments.

Many of my clients think they should wait before talking to their employees. Approaching an employee whose work effort needs to be corrected is uncomfortable. Waiting seems easier, but usually not the best choice. In supervision, the consequence of inaction is no action.

"Why don't you discuss this with your employee?"

𝒞 *I'm giving her time to improve.*
I hear this often. "If you're keeping this a secret, how much time do you plan to give your employee to figure out what she needs to do to improve?" I ask. This is not the perspective my client had in mind and the question sends a clear message. Your employee probably won't improve without your help. Employees need your help as soon as possible. This way you both succeed.

𝒞 *I'm not sure what she's doing is really all that bad, so I am waiting.*
"What are you specifically waiting for?" is my usual follow-up question. Poor performance builds mistake upon mistake. Fix it as soon as you can. Again, you both win.

☙ *I'm afraid I will hurt his feelings.*
Unless you plan to outright insult your
employee, my guess is that his feelings will
be hurt even more when you have to put him
on probation and he has no idea how he got
there. If you are unsure about how to provide
constructive criticism, practice with someone
you trust. If you would rather, write down your
thoughts and read them until you are comfortable. Try that. Choose your words carefully, get
feedback and then practice before you approach
your employee. Criticism that is constructive
and focused on the specific work effort is usually
well received.

☙ *I don't want to get angry or I don't want her to get
angry.*
Of course you need to be calm. Take ten, prepare
your talking points and set an example of being
able to discuss difficult subjects calmly. Sometimes a calm approach by you will diffuse her
anger and instill confidence that this will be a
rational discussion. If that isn't happening, postpone the meeting and explain what you expect
in an hour or whatever timeframe you like. Do
not postpone this for long. When dealing with a
volatile employee, or if you haven't had enough
experience with these types of conversations, it
can be helpful to bring in your manager, or a
human resource professional, for support.

꙲ *I am afraid.*
Of what? If you feel afraid to pull your employee aside to discuss a very small slice of the day, (because that's what it will be if you address the issue right away), you may want to work with an experienced manager or human resource professional to help develop your confidence in dealing with these situations.

꙲ *If I wait long enough she'll figure it out and quit.*
This type of reply is very concerning because, like the, *"I'm afraid,"* excuse, it suggests that the supervisor lacks the confidence or skills necessary to deal with difficult employee situations. The goal of uncomfortable conversations is to help the employee succeed. It is important that you find the tools to help you help your employee.

꙲ *I am waiting for him to make enough mistakes so I can put him on probation.* (Put more bluntly, and as one manager told me, *I'm waiting for him to dig his own hole so I can fire him).*
Really? I don't know about you, but this feels mean to me. Going from mistake to probation is harsh and is not likely to help the employee improve. As a human resource professional, I am highly suspect of a supervisor's skills if the goal is probation without having provided constructive feedback and training. Some employees can take longer to learn a skill or seem to resist authority, but it is your responsibility to provide the training and coaching necessary to succeed.

This means that, at times, you may be frustrated or irritated. But remember that if they succeed, so will you.

🐾 Finally, … *I don't know what to say or how to say it.*

We'll work on that next...

Keep this in mind:

Very few employees wake up in the morning and say to themselves, *"Let me see how I can really mess up today."*

∾

Most people want to succeed. If you keep that in mind when you approach an employee who needs assistance, you might find the conversations easier. Perhaps the most satisfying experience you will have as supervisor is seeing an employee, after a struggle with performance, become a positive and productive employee. It does happen.

Conversation starters:

John, do you have a minute?

If he is available, invite him to your office or a private place for further discussion, which can go like this: *I have been reviewing some of the results, and I see an error in the first part of the project. I'd like to review this with you.* Now you can begin an interactive discussion.

Takia, do you have a minute?

Again, invite Takia to your office or a private place for further discussion. *I'd like to review this report with you.*

Sam, do you have a minute?

Move to a private space and continue. *I want to talk to you about your work schedule. I have noticed that you have been late most days this week. Can you tell me what the problem is?* You're now ready to listen and begin an interactive discussion.

What are the common factors to each approach?

1. The supervisor is clearly stating the topic of concern.

2. The supervisor is seeking clarity from the employee.

3. The supervisor is seeking the right time for discussion.

4. The supervisor is conveying a sense that a mutual goal is employee success.

This is when active listening is critically important. Maybe *you* made a mistake in the scheduling or the assignment. This might be embarrassing, but fixable if you listen first. When you approach your employee with a sense that you are really interested in figuring this out, your chances of success are greatly improved. The conversation will flow naturally.

The conversation needs to be clear, direct and without drama

Start the conversation with a sense of direction in a neutral tone for the best chance of employee engagement. Offer an environment where the employee is willing to participate in the discussion.

- Hear his point of view.

- Learn the facts.

- Did he know he was making a mistake?

- Did he have enough information or training to succeed?

- Do you know what caused deficiency?

It's a good practice to summarize what was said. Now, don't get squirrely on me here. I am not suggesting that you take out that big nasty pad and make notes and demand a written apology from the employee. A simple summary comment, such as, "So, you will proof your worksheet before sending it to me and review the results with the senior tech before finalizing everything." That's it. Follow this with, "Let me know if you need any further help with this."

The Conversation:

- ✓ State your concern clearly.

- ✓ Ask questions to guide the conversation toward the information you need.

- ✓ Work toward solving the problem rather than laying blame.

- ✓ Include an agreement on actions to take.

- ✓ End with an offer to help.

∽

After you conclude the meeting with your employee, make notes of what was said. Date your notes. Good record keeping is essential. You won't remember the details several days or weeks later when you follow up with the employee.

NOTES:

Follow-up

Always follow up. If you never mention the meeting again, you lose the opportunity to discuss success. "Good job" will go a long way in keeping things on track.

However, if success doesn't follow your efforts, the follow-up meeting becomes an essential part of the performance management process. Not following up means that it will be much more difficult at the next step.

What can happen if I don't meet with my employee?

Not providing feedback along the way means that nothing is really being managed. You are letting the employee float along until success or failure happens with very little sense of direction. Good for her if she succeeds but if she fails, she will be held accountable. Is the failure entirely her fault?

I have a story I'd like to share with you. Sadly, the story is all too common.

I was consulting for a small manufacturing firm near a large city. I was asked to coach a supervisor, Jake, who had just been thrust into this new role. He had not formally supervised employees, so coaching was requested by his manager to help him succeed.

One of the people Jake would supervise was someone who had formerly been a peer. This can be difficult for a new supervisor. Hillary, who had been with the company longer than Jake, was transferred from another department to work under Jake. They were acquainted with each other through company functions.

Hillary was not happy with the transfer and Jake sensed it. By the time I met with Jake, things had gone from bad to worse. They weren't speaking at all. I asked if Jake was intimidated by the situation, and he said he was. "I just don't know how to approach Hillary without seeming bossy or like a know-it-all."

We discussed the issue and Jake agreed that he should probably make an effort to meet with Hillary, even briefly, without getting into work details. I suggested he just start with friendly greetings and small talk on Hillary's turf for the week. Remember Verbal Rule # 1: "At least say hello." The goal for Jake and Hillary was to get comfortable with each other. Jake said that he would have no problems doing that and I got a commitment from him that he would proceed.

After three weeks of cancelling our coaching meetings, I got the message that Jake was not comfortable after all. I reported the cancellations to his manager and encouraged him to discuss the situation further with Jake. I was happy to resume coaching, if Jake would like.

While I continued to work in other areas of the company, I did not interact with any of them directly again until I received a call from Jake's senior manager, who asked to meet with me to discuss a "delicate situation." At that meeting I learned about a situation concerning Jake, Hillary, and Gavin, the unit manager. During the interim period, Gavin had inserted himself into supervising Hillary. He had not encouraged Jake to resume coaching or even modify how he worked with Hillary. In the end, Gavin demoted Hillary and put her on probation. Hillary had received no warning. She was simply told that, she "had an attitude and was unwilling to work in a team environment." Everyone agreed that Hillary was, "uncooperative and a problem for everyone with her constant complaining."

A review of Hillary's history with the company indicated that her performance appraisals had been excellent under prior supervisors. Hillary had never displayed much project initiative, but this wasn't expected at her level of professional development. She kept to herself in the other departments where she worked, but there was no suggestion that she was a deficient performer. Some people told me that Hillary was shy and reserved, not into smiling or mingling. She apparently liked working at the company, but didn't demonstrate that openly.

Hillary met with her unit director to complain about the demotion and probation. She got little clarification and never saw the director after that one meeting. Not much later, Hillary's employment was terminated for "deficient performance."

Hillary sued the company for well over $200,000 and claimed that she was fired in retaliation for complaining to the unit director. Everyone shook their head and agreed they were right all along. Hillary was a problem employee. I had the sense that those involved felt vindicated.

I was beginning to think of Host Jibibbi Not-So-Much.

Senior management drew me into this situation shortly after Hillary had complained to her unit director. I heard comments like, "We did everything we could, she had a chance to improve, and she was affecting the morale of everyone in the unit." The discussion, which included the unit director and Jake, revealed that no one had reached out to Hillary at any time except to discuss the probation. "Hillary had the skills to be successful in the new project, but she just didn't cut it." That was as specific as anyone would get during my meeting with the group.

These managers and supervisors still have difficulty seeing beyond "Hillary's surly attitude." Her lawsuit was described as "frivolous" and there was general agreement that they did "the right thing by firing her."

Hillary won a considerable settlement because the law was on her side.

Terminating an employee after she complains to management can be seen in the courts as retaliation. As a supervisor, it is important that you have labor law knowledge and understand how your supervision of employees relates to the company's legal obligations. Ignoring employee concerns can have serious consequences down the road.

This is more than a legal issue, however. It's an example of performance management gone awry. If Hillary's supervisor had established a productive working relationship with her and/or the unit director had intervened, this company might not be writing such a large check to a former employee.

When you think you "did everything right," it's easy to get upset when someone sues. It's harder to find your own responsibility in the event.

Reviewing the events, whose fault was this mess? See any Jibibbi I-Got-Your-Backs in this story?

Can you list at least one thing each of these employees did to contribute to Hillary's successful lawsuit?

Supervisor _____

Unit director _____

Departmental director _____

∾

Before you blame your employee, ask yourself these questions:

- ↝ *Am I treating my employees the way I want to be treated?*

- ↝ *Am I helping my employees learn their jobs?*

- ↝ *Am I helping my employees improve?*

- ↝ *Am I telling my employees how they are doing?*

Common performance issues

To succeed at performance management, a supervisor must distinguish between the employee's work performance and behavior. Work performance is easy to document, describe, and measure. When this is the only problem – deficient performance on an assigned project – it is usually easier to discuss. Provided the employee understands what is expected, the performance deficiency often reflects lack of training and experience. Skill training is often effective in improving work performance.

Problems with an employee's behavior in the work place are a different issue. This is touchier and more difficult to handle. Behavior is harder to measure and isolate because it's personal. If an employee needs to correct professional behavior, it comes down to you. Your ability as a supervisor to describe the behavior you observe, rather than offer a generalized statement about the person, is important. For example, if you have an employee who has difficulty working as part of your team, telling him that he is "not a team player" is less effective than describing certain behaviors such as frequent arguing, not volunteering for those "extra duties," and not attending staff meetings. Saying, "you're not a team player," invites defensiveness. Describing what you observe as isolated incidences and inviting discussion increases the likelihood of an interactive discussion and resolution. You're not branding the employee; you're trying to understand what's going on.

"My employees complain about the slackers."

I was once a consultant for an emerging company with progressive management. Benefits flowed freely, managers were flexible, (almost) everyone worked hard, and the work product was important. Wow, this was impressive. I wanted to learn more about the corporate culture, morale and general employee welfare, so I asked to meet with employees in groups by general level of employment (the organizational structure was fairly flat, but everyone "knew their place"). It didn't take long to unearth general resentment of the management team and suffering morale. I heard words like "unfair" frequently, but not in the expected context. What was unfair was that, "Slackers got away with stuff all the time." This theme repeated itself from group to group – and with increasing animosity. Word was out that I was listening, so tell it like it is.

I dug deeper with an employee satisfaction survey. The results were telling. While the employees were glad to be working for such "nice people," management's inability to correct the poor performance of a few was having a serious impact on everyone. Repeatedly, employees said that, "The slackers were in charge." This diminished many of the positive aspects of working for this company and injected a generous dose of unfairness into the work environment. Good intentions gone bad.

I offered percentages of dissatisfaction and specific complaints in writing using the survey results as a foundation. The managers were shocked. "We were just being nice. How many slackers do we have anyway? You can't just go and fire people." Hmm. This may take a while to work through.

The well-meaning managers believed addressing poor performance or terminating employment was morally wrong or "mean." They didn't understand how letting the slackers continue to underperform would affect the morale of their best, or even satisfactory, employees.

Even if you don't fully succeed in improving the performance of deficient employees, your efforts will be noticed and appreciated by the others. Trying is a good first step.

"My employee is always late."

Employee tardiness is a problem that you might have to deal with.

All new employees need to know your expectations for time and attendance. Some of them may have come from more flexible environments. Recent grads are used to showing up for class when they want and some haven't yet been trained on why getting to work on time is critical. You need to set the standard. If you don't, that's *your first* deficiency.

You have to set the stage. The first day that Ben is late, you need to have a conversation. Remember – always address the issue right away.

Here's how it goes. "Ben, I noticed you came in at 9:00 this morning. I was counting on you being here at 8:30. Can you tell me why you were late? What happened?"

Make sure you understand Ben's perspective. Earlier, we discussed the possible ramifications of not understanding the employee's perspective. You don't want to miss those extenuating circumstances that require your compassion.

However, let's assume that Ben has a history of coming to work late. You know he understands the policy and you know that he does not have issues that prevent him from arriving on time because you asked him during your previous conversations.

Here's the way I have handled tardiness. Late once, life happens. Address the problem. Late twice, be on alert and give clear notice of expectations. Late three times requires more – a clear message of consequences. Find your way, make it clear and be consistent.

If this is a chronic problem, here are some conversations starters to consider. You can still apply the principles of asking questions.

"Ben, this is the third time in two weeks that you have arrived late to work. What's going on?"

"Will you be able to be here on time? Is there a way to work this out?"

"Do you understand the policy that, if you are late again, I will need to submit a disciplinary note to your personnel file?

"Do I have your commitment to arriving on time?"

There's no lecturing here. Ben has been given another chance to explain the situation. The supervisor has warned him of the consequences and Ben has been given the opportunity to confirm that he understands.

Be certain to follow through with the consequences.

This is what your employee gets out of this – if I am late, consideration is given to my situation. If I don't correct my deficiencies, there will be consequences. Your employees will likely respond well to these steps because they seem fair. Everyone has the same requirement to be at work on time.

If Ben improves, tell him that you have noticed. Not a big deal, but it reinforces his improvement and closes the topic.

Keep in mind that if your company has a flex work schedule option, that can resolve legitimate issues some people have with work hours. Explore this option.

"My employee's work is sloppy and inaccurate."

What if someone has a problem with a job-required task? It's inaccurate, incomplete, late, or thin in substance. This often means that your employee needs more training. It's pretty easy to identify and quantify work performance deficiencies.

Fallon had just been promoted to supervisor. Her promotion was largely based on her superior technical skills with very little consideration to her professional maturity or confidence. Fallon had much to learn as a new supervisor, and her first challenge related to a subordinate, Yolanda. Yolanda was sloppy with the organization of her scanning projects. Her documents were not facing the same direction, the folders for storage weren't right, and pages were skipped. Her work performance was seriously deficient. Fallon made assumptions that Yolanda was doing this on purpose. Soon these deficiencies felt like a personal affront. When I first discussed this with Fallon, she was emotional. She was so skilled at this task that she simply couldn't imagine someone having so many problems with it. "It's just so easy," she told me somewhat angrily. After some discussion and cooling down, Fallon agreed to ask Yolanda how she thought she was doing with the project. To her surprise, Fallon discovered that Yolanda had never been trained. She was put on the project by the prior supervisor and that was the end of any interaction (Jibibbi Host Not-So-Much, I'm thinking?). Basically, Yolanda was winging it and she was very uncomfortable about that. Fallon offered training and in no time Yolanda's performance improved. By approaching Yolanda with an open mind and a willingness to help, she responded well. The performance deficiency turned around quickly and Yolanda soon became one of Fallon's biggest supporters during her transition to supervisor.

Things don't always go so easily. However, they will likely be easier than you have imagined, especially if you deal with issues right away.

Remember these tips:

- ✓ If you see deficient performance, speak up.

- ✓ Tell your employee – in private – what specific task or action is deficient and specifically how it needs to improve.

- ✓ Talk to the person how you'd like someone to speak with you.

- ✓ Ask for his/her perspective or concern.

- ✓ Ask how you can help. If an employee needs training, provide it.

- ✓ Meet periodically to provide progress.

- ✓ Ask for feedback from the employee to gauge how he or she sees progress moving.

- ✓ If helpful, offer additional assistance.

- ✓ When success is evident, share that.

"I don't like his behavior."

Unprofessional or inappropriate behavior is difficult to quantify. However, if behavior is really deficient, it's not difficult to describe. Supervisors need to know how to describe the deficient and expected behavior. Employees with subpar behavior often need coaching or mentoring. Be prepared to work on this with patience and persistence.

Many supervisors have more trouble with correcting behavior than task performance. Addressing behavior seems personal and feels uncomfortable. It might remind us of conflict with someone in our family or personal life. When that happens, emotions creep in and we get intimidated with the task at hand. It's easier to ignore the issue. Of course, it doesn't go away and often gets worse.

Think about the grouch who comes to work a bit late every day, sneers at co-workers and sits down without so much as a howdy-do. The grouch never volunteers for those "other duties" and is quick to anger when co-workers call her on it. She does her work, but only at the most basic level. Everyone begins to avoid her, including you. Who wants to be around this? You are the supervisor and *you* are allowing one person to make everyone else's day at work uncomfortable. The longer you allow this behavior, the likelier it will affect other employees. They will be upset with *you*. Uh oh.

First line supervision is the most difficult job in the company. Why? Because it *is* more personal – more is asked of you because you have to effect changes in people to achieve the goals. We need to change gears as supervisors and realize that these issues can't be handled like our personal lives – you know, have that good old fashioned family argument. Hug later. Nope. Regardless of your professional credentials or years of experience, accept that this job has uncomfortable moments. Expect that. When you observe unprofessional behavior you need to <u>learn how to describe the behavior you see</u> and <u>describe the behavior you expect</u>. You have to explain how your employee's behavior is affecting other employees and how it affects the team as a whole. This may be hard to do the first time, but this skill develops quickly with practice.

Preparing for performance discussions minimizes discomfort.

"She has an attitude!"

I've heard this many times. What the heck is that? It's used in so many contexts and described in so many different ways that if someone told me I had an attitude I wouldn't know whether to be happy or insulted. The word "attitude" represents a group of behaviors. Are we handling a difficult situation with guts or are we rude and dismissive?

If a supervisor tells me that an employee has an "attitude," I ask for a description of behavior. This is where we start – by describing behavior, not by making sweeping generalities. Now the supervisor describes an em-

78

ployee who "is dismissive of other people's ideas, ignores requests from me, thinks she is always right, and argues with everyone." These behaviors can be disruptive to the workplace and teamwork, which is critical for success. Once the supervisor is able to describe and focus on these specific behaviors, he can have a more productive discussion with the employee. The supervisor's goal is to use that information to help the employee see the consequences of behavior and make positive changes.

It won't surprise you if I say that, when you initiate this type of discussion with your employee, you may get some resistance. It is difficult to hear that your behavior is not acceptable. This is the uncomfortable part of the process. Who likes to be criticized, especially if it feels personal?

Guidelines for the 'difficult conversation'

Tell your employee what you see. Be specific. "Harriet, I have noticed that you have been arguing with other employees. Sometimes in meetings, you seem unhappy with the plans we put forward. It's having a negative, distracting impact on others. It's affecting the work we need to be doing. I have noticed this behavior for the past month, and want to discuss it with you."

Ask what's going on. "Is there something I need to be aware of or that I can help you with?" Give employees a chance to talk. "Harriet" may ramble, get upset, or act defensively, but she will get her chance to talk. Ask more questions, such as "Can you help me understand that better?" or "Do you mean that…?" if she needs help to move through the problem. These clarifying questions tell your employee that you are listening and that you want to understand the situation as she sees it. This will pay off big time as you work together to help her succeed.

If you find out that you need to broaden your conversation to include others, do so. However, let's assume she can't defend her behavior and it needs to change.

State your expectations

> "Charlene, it still doesn't make sense to me that you are arguing so frequently with others in the group. As I mentioned, this behavior is affecting morale and productivity. I realize you may disagree with Terrell from time to time, but how can you handle your disagreements more productively?"

Let's assume that Charlene is engaged in the conversation. You and she can then begin to identify ways she can work more effectively. Be specific and ask for specifics if she engages positively in the topic. Your chances for success will improve greatly if your employee participates, which will be easier for her to do if you have listened and have asked for suggestions. You are the supervisor, however, so your expectations need to be clear to her at the end of your conversation. Summarize the conversation and future actions.

Work out a time line for improving and ask if she has any questions or issues that need further discussion. How can you help?

When the conversation ends, I encourage supervisors to get a commitment from their employees that their behavior will change. "Can I count on you to make every effort to improve in this area?" Let Charlene know you are available if she needs any additional suggestions that will help her work better with Terrell. Remember to follow up.

∾

At work, one person's behavior will affect everyone else so we need the best from everyone. The person with the most difficult behavior will have the strongest influence on the morale of the group.

It is up to the supervisor to take the lead. You will have to deal with deficient behavior from your employees. This is never easy. However, in addition to having a negative effect on your team, the consequences of not dealing with deficiencies in your group will ultimately make you look bad – not a good thing.

t should be done?

)efine the unacceptable behavior.

2. Ask the employee about the behavior.

3. Define what acceptable behavior is.

4. Seek suggestions from employee as to how to change or modify behavior.

5. Ask how you can help.

6. Provide a summary of all relevant suggestions for improving behavior.

7. Get a commitment to improve.

Follow up:

1. Tell the employee to talk to you if she has a problem and mean it.

2. Be available if further assistance is requested and mentor or coach as needed.

3. Meet periodically to get and give feedback.

4. When success is evident, speak up.

NOTES:

I worked the program, but nothing changed.

There are challenging employees in every company. Some individuals resist authority, and it might seem impossible to establish a productive working relationship with these employees. Some individuals are not meant for the job. It's simply not a good fit. As a supervisor, you will likely manage one or more of these types of employees along the way. Is there a magic supervisory tool to fix such a resistive employee, get cooperation and improve performance? No, but let's outline a plan.

Accept that you will not be able to improve or effectively manage everyone's performance. It doesn't necessarily imply failure on your part.

If you have made every attempt to help your employee and are not seeing positive results, seek assistance. If you have an active and engaged human resources program, head there first.

Human resource pros are there to help resolve management issues and handle conflict. It is also the job of human resources to identify "red flags." Sometimes, when an employee's performance and behavior is questionable and difficult to manage, you can make mistakes. You do not want to plow through with a deficient employee, end up in a termination meeting and learn later that some of your actions resulted in legal problems for the company. If you do not have a human resource department, work your way up the organizational chain. Find an experienced manager to guide you with these difficult situations.

When you meet with a human resource or senior management professional, she will want assurance that you have actually met with your employee and discussed performance expectations and deficiencies.

Make sure you are familiar with your company's policies before proceeding with formal disciplinary meetings with an employee.

When an employee is not improving, and taking into account corporate policy, a Performance Improvement Plan will often be drafted. This process involves you and an HR pro or senior manager formalizing the correction process and providing written documentation to the employee detailing what the expectations are, what the consequences will be and a timeline for improvement.

❧

ritten performance plan includes:

1. A description of the deficient performance.

2. A description of what constitutes satisfactory performance with clear expectations of performance.

3. Available training and mentoring as necessary.

4. A reasonable time frame (perhaps a month) for improvement.

5. Follow up dates with the employee.

6. Specific consequences will be noted if performance does not improve within the agreed upon timeline.

7. Both you and the employee will sign and date this plan and commit to your respective responsibilities.

This process gives you and the employee time for fair assessment and conclusions. This Performance Improvement Plan should only occur after you have had informal meetings with the employee and provided time to improve. No one should be surprised when a Performance Improvement Plan is initiated. Surprise may send the disciplined, disgruntled employee to a senior executive or, worse, a lawyer. Never surprise your employee.

Performance Improvement Plans are significant employee actions. The original signed document is usually placed in the employee's personnel file. You need to ensure closure – successful or not. If the employee is successful, that needs to be formally noted in the personnel file. If the employee isn't successful, management will want documentation that the process was completed as agreed.

In the final analysis…

Some deficient employees improve and move forward as productive contributors. However, if someone has not been responsive to correction and coaching and you need to put them on a Performance Improvement Plan, the odds may no longer be in their favor. This company may not be a good fit. If termination is recommended and initiated, that is the perspective I impart. Some people and companies are just not a good fit. Let them go.

Performance management is not an easy process. It is a constant in the supervisor's professional life but should not be construed to be a negative. Effective performance management includes training enthusiastic employees and working with individuals on your team who are demonstrating professional growth and initiative. In essence, effective performance management is helping positive employees plan and implement their career paths. This is one of the best parts of the job. Enjoy it.

Unfortunately, it's the challenging employees who consume much of our time and energies. I wish there were some magic bullets for you in these cases. There really aren't any. However, there are tools to increase the odds of success for you and your employee. Some will work with certain employees and some will not. There are no guarantees. Just remember that most employees want to succeed and do well. Give them your best shot.

NOTES:

Performance Management Tools to Manage the Challenging Employee

- Meet with your employee about your concerns as soon as possible.

- Clearly describe what you see and know.

- Ask questions and listen.

- Offer assistance to help the employee succeed.

- Follow up. Follow up. Follow up.

- Know your company policies and seek assistance if you need to take corrective action.

- Provide closure whether the employee succeeds or not.

∾

If the employee is not able to improve, you may need to conclude that he or she is not a good fit for the company. Sometimes it's just that – not a good fit.

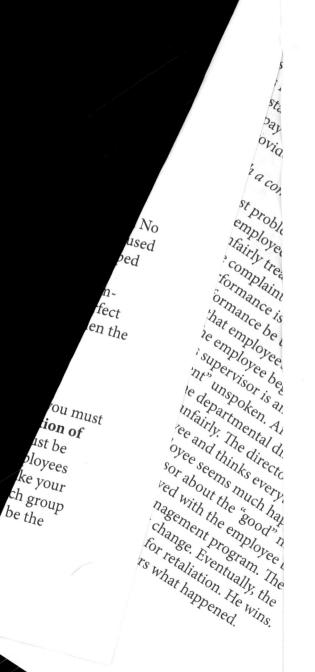

There are occasions in the life of a human resource professional and supervisor when a personnel situation has the potential to develop into a serious legal problem for a company. I call these "red flag" situations. A red flag situation is when an employee, regardless of performance or behavior, feels aggrieved or unfairly treated. This sense of distress or injustice can be real or imagined depending on your perspective. It doesn't matter. What matters is how you handle it and that you handle it quickly and legally. The longer a supervisor waits to manage a discontented employee, the more likely that discontentment will result in a big problem.

I received two calls in one week that highlight this topic. The first call came from Jacob, the founder and president of a home security company, who wanted to know how he could reduce lawsuits against his firm. In the span of twelve years, Jacob's firm had grown from seven employees to over two hundred. Jacob was proud of the type of company he had established. He had worked hard to create an employee-friendly environment and had provided well for his employees in terms of salary, benefits and corporate culture. The increase in legal actions against the company was confusing him. We agreed that I should meet with some of his supervisors to figure out what's happening. These meetings were enlightening. I learned that, in addition to weak supervisory skills, Jacob's supervisors had virtually no understanding of basic labor law. Many of the supervisors were managing inconsistently and sometimes giving preference to one employee over another for vague

...e. Of course, in these situations, some empl...
...at the supervisors were unfair. When an...
...her employee describes inconsistent m...
...d a sense that supervisors favor one...
another at work, a jury may agree...
to fix this problem. Red flags...
them.

The second call ca...
devices compa...
time. "Ra...
her supervi...
manager. She...
pened. "I don't...
for help." Red fla...

What to do when con...

🕯 *Kno...*

It's crucial for you to understa...
laws. These laws set standards o...
protect employees from employm...
When a supervisor is unaware of th...
the company may become vulnerable...
seen claims of a violation of an employe...
crimination, hostile work environment, re...
other similar offenses because managers and...
were ignorant of labor law. **Ignorance is not a...
when you face a judge and jury.**

Usually, your company handbook provides informa...

What happened was the supervisor didn't take the complaint seriously.

✓ She did not actively listen to determine what
needed to be done to move the employee's focus
to his performance rather than deciding he was
simply being treated unfairly.

✓ The supervisor did not tell her manager.

✓ The manager did not work with or guide the
supervisor after meeting with the employee.

✓ The employee felt upset because the manager
never seemed to act upon his complaint.

In the end, the employee felt he was fired because he...
had complained to the director about the supervisor...
one had really listened to the employee who was foc...
solely on how he was being treated. No one had hel...
the employee reconcile his complaint and move the...
focus back to improving work performance. The e...
ployee's sense of unfairness festered. This is the pe...
storm for a retaliation suit. The red flag waved wh...
employee first complained to his supervisor.

🕯 *Be consistent with employee actions*

To reduce the likelihood of a red flag situation,...
**provide consistent messages and implementa...
policies to all employees.** Corrective action m...
applied equitably. You probably have some em...
who are high maintenance and others who ma...
day run smoothly but, if an employee from ea...
comes late to work, the actions you take mus...
...ame.

about the protections available to all employees. Read this section and understand these protections so you can give these to each employee you supervise. If you have questions about how the law applies, talk to your company's human resource professional or a manager who understand these laws. Ask for training in this area. It will pay off big time for the company if labor law training is provided to all supervisors and managers.

₢ Deal with a complaint of unfairness *immediately*

This is the biggest problem I deal with. The scenario goes like this: an employee complains to the supervisor that he feels unfairly treated. The supervisor listens but doesn't take the complaint seriously because the employee's work performance is so bad. How can correcting deficient performance be unfair? The supervisor continues to manage that employee's work performance in the same fashion. The employee begins to tell all of his peers how unfair his supervisor is and leaves no detail of this "poor treatment" unspoken. After a while, the employee complains to the departmental director that his supervisor treats him unfairly. The director has "a good chat" with the employee and thinks everything has been fixed because the employee seems much happier. The director tells the supervisor about the "good" meeting. The supervisor gets annoyed with the employee but continues the performance management program. The employee's performance doesn't change. Eventually, the employee is terminated. He sues for retaliation. He wins. Management calls me and wonders what happened.

What happened was the supervisor didn't take the complaint seriously.

- ✓ She did not actively listen to determine what needed to be done to move the employee's focus to his performance rather than deciding he was simply being treated unfairly.
- ✓ The supervisor did not tell her manager.
- ✓ The manager did not work with or guide the supervisor after meeting with the employee.
- ✓ The employee felt upset because the manager never seemed to act upon his complaint.

In the end, the employee <u>felt</u> he was fired because he had complained to the director about the supervisor. No one had really listened to the employee who was focused solely on how he was being treated. No one had helped the employee reconcile his complaint and move the focus back to improving work performance. The employee's sense of unfairness festered. This is the perfect storm for a retaliation suit. The red flag waved when the employee first complained to his supervisor.

ℰ *Be consistent with employee actions*

To reduce the likelihood of a red flag situation, you must **provide consistent messages and implementation of policies to all employees**. Corrective action must be applied equitably. You probably have some employees who are high maintenance and others who make your day run smoothly but, if an employee from each group comes late to work, the actions you take must be the same.

Just a quick point here: Some people require more time and training. This is just a fact. Get used to it. You may have to manage their performance with more attention than employees who require less of your time and energy, but the standards of performance you expect must be the same.

𝕔 Provide consistent messages

Make sure there is a **consistency of message up the line of authority**. If the supervisor begins corrective action and the manager changes course and retracts that corrective action, problems – not of the employee's making – will arise. A supervisor should have the ducks in a row before taking any corrective action. Make sure your manager agrees and that follow-through will be supported.

𝕔 Manage wth fairness

Your employees are not your friends or family where you can pick favorites to go to the game with you. **At work, regardless of how you feel about someone, all employees are entitled to fair treatment.**

If there is a lawsuit, management usually neglected the supervisory work that needed to be done. There are frivolous lawsuits. However, a skilled supervisor with good support from management can prevent most lawsuits. The *perception* of fairness can be more important than the reality. Listen to your employees. Understand their reality and help them understand that they *are* being treated fairly.

You can minimize red flag situations by:

* Knowing labor laws
* Dealing with difficult situations immediately
* Acting consistently among all employees
* Listening to your employees
* Sending a consistent message to all employees
* Managing all employees with fairness

❧

Remember that the perception of truth is as important as the actual truth. It is critical that you recognize your employee's perception of the truth and not the truth as *you* see it.

Micromanagement

There should be a support group for micromanagers. It could be called MMA – micromanagers anonymous. Micromanagers come in all sizes and shapes; there are many of them and they are everywhere. I can pick out a micromanager during one brief interaction. I hear the clue words the way a master piano tuner can tell when a note is flat. There is no escaping me. Why? Because I am a recovering MMA-er.

I used to call myself a "fixer" but when micromanagers say this, they just think no one else can fix "it" as well as they can. The "fixer" or micromanager can tell you what's wrong, what *you* are doing wrong, how *you* should improve what you are doing and, after you correct *your* problem, the micromanager will follow your every move to ensure your continued success. Aren't we great?

It's rewarding to think we have control. However, we rarely have the control we think we do. Micromanagement is a common characteristic in new or untrained supervisors. We think that if we can control the situation, we'll have a better chance of succeeding in our job. Unfortunately, if you are on the receiving end of a micromanager, success is the last thing you will feel.

It's all about the trust

Micromanagers want to control the work environment to guarantee success that they fear won't happen without their fingerprints on every project and process. Often, micromanagers lack the confidence that the staff wants to do well or they think the employees don't have the competence to do the job well. This can translate into the need to control the work so the micromanager can feel success or accomplishment through his individual effort. It hasn't occurred to the MMA-er that this strategy actually decreases staff efforts. A micromanaged employee senses pretty quickly when a supervisor doesn't trust that the work will be done "right." The more the supervisor micromanages, the more he is proving to himself that he is right – "These people need to be managed carefully."

Sadly, in the work environment, a micromanager sends one primary message to the staff: "I don't trust you."

I recall a grants administrator, Stephanie, who complained bitterly about her micromanaging supervisor. "I used to love what I was doing before I had to work with Megan. It was fun just coming to work where I got to work on various projects and interface with a lot of people. I used to feel so good about what I was doing. People liked my work. I loved working here. Now, I just hate going to work. Every day I feel like a failure," she said. "Megan gives me projects and then wastes so much of my time sending reminder emails or suggestions for getting this or that done. She complains that I don't keep her in the loop. She is the loop – she makes the loop and she ties the loop. What can I tell her that she hasn't already told me to do? I'm trying to find a new job. The problem," she said, "is that there aren't many openings in my line of work. I need the money, so I just suck it up." Stephanie was miserable. She had given up. I was pretty sure that, in time, Megan would be citing her for deficient work performance. How tragic.

I knew Megan. I also knew she had a high regard for Stephanie and was really looking forward to this new assignment and working with such a high performer. Of course, this wasn't evident at all to Stephanie. Things went downhill fast. I wasn't Megan's coach, but I touched base sometimes to see how things were going. Despite some efforts on my part, it was clear that Megan had a serious blind spot when it came to supervision style. She was unable to see how her micromanagement was affecting all of her staff. Eventually, the entire unit was underperforming. Megan's enthusiasm for her new job diminished and her confidence was waning. She asked for a transfer. What could have been a win-win for this enthusiastic group of people fell apart quickly under the dreary cloud of micromanagement.

Truisms about micromanagement that every new supervisor needs to know...

* Micromanagement is not an effective tool for improving an employee's performance

* It does not ensure the success of the projects or processes

* It conveys a sense of distrust in the employee's ability to do a good job

* It results in decreased morale

❧

I have coached many supervisors who tell me right away that they aren't micromanagers. "I know micromanagement. I have seen it and I hated it when it happened to me. I won't do that to someone else," one client told me emphatically. Having suffered under a micromanager isn't a vaccine. You are not immune to becoming a micromanager. Things are different when you get in the supervisor's chair.

The difference between effective management and micromanagement

Effective management requires the willingness to delegate work. To properly delegate, a supervisor needs to trust the employees' ability and willingness to do a good job. This isn't easy because the supervisor will need to:

- ✎ *be able to assess each employee's skill sets and level of ability in various work areas.*

- ✎ *understand the employee's willingness to assume responsibility for the assignment.*

- ✎ *realize the employee's willingness to work well with the team.*

- ✎ *know the employee's ability to accomplish tasks in a timely fashion.*

If the supervisor has developed the skill to make these assessments, she is prepared to delegate work projects. This frees her up to *manage* these projects rather than perform every task at hand.

When micromanagers don't trust employees' abilities or willingness to complete projects "properly," they feel the need to check in frequently (ahem, all the time). They monitor the work product. They don't ask employees' opinions and listening isn't a strong suit. Micromanagers often take credit for the work and feel deserving of this credit because they've "had to work so hard with the employee to get it done right." "Thank you," and, "Good job" are phrases not often heard from micromanagers.

Delegating and trusting your employees' capabilities are two of the most essential management tools.

Remember these critical elements for improving your grasp of these supervisory tools:

- ✓ The effective supervisor <u>wants employees to succeed</u>.

- ✓ A good supervisor <u>understands the strengths and challenges of each employee</u> so that the work assigned is appropriate to each employee's skill level.

- ✓ A successful supervisor <u>trusts that employees are ready for the assigned work</u> and trusts that the employee will ask for assistance when needed. With care, the supervisor lets them fail so they can learn.

- ✓ The skilled supervisor <u>seeks an employee's input and encourages dialogue</u>.

- ✓ These supervisors <u>listen</u>.

- ✓ They let employees make mistakes, but <u>know when to offer help</u> so the mistakes can be corrected quickly and in a productive fashion.

- ✓ They help employees <u>learn how to improve and develop skills.</u>

- ✓ They <u>allow employees to make decisions appropriate to the assignments.</u>

- ✓ They <u>trust employees</u> and the employees can clearly sense that.

- ✓ They <u>reward an employee's success</u> – "Good job" and "Thank you" are valued.

"I'm just helping"

Most of the supervisors I meet want to do well. They also *think* they want their employees to succeed. Unfortunately, micromanaging supervisors have a tendency to "help" when it isn't really needed. Usually, it is hugely overbearing. A supervisor I coached a few years back typified this type of management. Joani was a smiling and concerned manager who, soon after we met, told me about a troubling issue. All of the employees she trained and nurtured to promotion as supervisors ended up leaving her unit or the company within a year of that promotion. "It's like when I promote them, they turn on me. After they are promoted, I feel like they hate me for some reason. I just want to help them and they don't appreciate a thing. Did they just use me when they were learning stuff?" Joani was deeply upset and demoralized.

I asked Joani for some examples of how she helped her new supervisors. She told me about Adam, who was recently promoted. Adam worked in the quality control section of Joani's unit. While he seemed to be doing a good job managing the workflow and testing protocols, Joani said that Adam "was not carefully monitoring

some of his employees' work, particularly the end processes." Joani decided to send emails to the employees
Adam was not "disciplining" for sloppiness. Joani copied
Adam "so he could see how to discipline for shoddy
work. I am just trying to help Adam. He's a new supervisor and needs to be firmer about the end process QC
work." Frankly, I was horrified that Joani was sending
corrective emails to Adam's employees. Joani was clueless as to how this might affect Adam. "After all, I'm just
helping him."

Here we have a manager who trains worthy employees
to be eligible for promotion to supervisor in her department. When the promotion comes, she inserts herself
into their supervisory work without any prior discussion. And she wonders what went wrong.

When you think you are helping or training your employees and there is resistance, it's time to look at your
own behavior and ask, "Am I micromanaging?"

Don't confuse micromanagement with training

A lot of new supervisors tell me that they aren't micromanaging, they are training the staff. Usually, when I ask
for specific information on the training program, I get
that "uh oh" look. Turns out the micromanager is telling
and tracking more than training. If you have a training
program, make it a training program. Set up a training
program that includes goals, skills to learn, and communication systems. Be clear that you are training. If
you are checking everyone's work or directing everyone's
day, you are likely micromanaging.

Tips to help avoid micromanaging

There are two critical assumptions you need to make to succeed at this:

> ➤ _Employees want to succeed as much as you do._

> ➤ _Your employees do not want you to fail._

Here are some ideas to help minimize your need to micromanage:

ℰ Shortly after starting your new position (or after you read this book), meet with your employees as a group. The purpose is to discuss work projects, progress, needs and openly ask for suggestions. This sets a positive tone for the employees and lets them know that you want to work with them as a team.

> ➤ Ask for suggestions to make the unit work well together and succeed. Ask how you can help.

> ➤ Set up regular group meetings to review projects, progress, and needs. Every meeting has an agenda, ideas are welcomed, action items are clear and there is follow-up. Follow-up – not tracking.

ℰ Next, set up individual meetings to learn about your employees' specific work, needs, goals, and progress. This will help you assess your employees' strengths and challenges.

- ➤ Ask for suggestions to help him/her succeed. Ask how you can help.

- ➤ Set up regular individual meetings to review progress, issues, goals and needs. Regular doesn't necessarily mean often. Set your schedule according to your needs and the needs of your employee. Just make them regular and something your employee can count on.

- ♗ If errors or delays are evident in group or individual efforts, arrange a meeting so the issues and solutions can be discussed. Do this as soon as possible. Just like in the section on performance management, it is important to clear up issues as quickly as possible.

- ♗ Avoid corrections via email since that rarely provides perspective or the training necessary to improve.

- ♗ Finally, expect success and communicate that expectation positively. If you don't believe that your employees will succeed, they will know it and you will likely revert to micromanagement.

After you use these tools, close your eyes and wait – you might be more happily surprised than you imagined.

Thoughts for MMA-ers:

* Trust your employees

* Delegate work effectively

* Avoid the blame game

* Avoid corrections by email

* Reward success

∾

Delegating

Do You Need to Delegate More?
Answer **Yes** or **No**:

- Do you regularly take work home?
- Do you work longer than your team members and others in the company?
- Do you sometimes have to do things that others should be doing for themselves?
- When you look at a task, do you seldom (if ever) think to ask yourself, "Could a member of my staff do this task for me?"
- When you return from an absence, is your "in" basket overflowing?
- Do you lack confidence in some of your team members?
- Are you still handling some of the same activities and problems before your last promotion?
- Are you constantly interrupted with questions for guidance by people who work for you?
- Are you still doing the routine details that others could be handling?
- Do you like to keep a finger in every pot?
- Do you rush to meet deadlines?
- Are you increasingly unable to keep on top of priorities?

If you answered yes to more than four questions, you need to learn about the benefits of delegating work.

For a micromanager, delegating is the scariest word in the English language. Delegate? "If I delegate some projects, who knows what will happen? It's best if I do the project myself." I have a very hard time getting micromanagers to delegate projects.

Let me tell you the difference between helping and delegating. Helping is when you ask someone to take some of the workload off of your shoulders. This is simply being a part of the workforce. Everyone is expected to pitch in when there is more work than you can handle. Helping might be filing, cleaning, faxing, completing forms, doing a bit more of the same task or bringing something to or from a place. You just need someone to give you a hand. Assistants help. That's their job – helping you with support tasks so you can get the projects completed. At some point, everyone helps someone else at work. It's expected. Micromanagers rarely have problems asking for help.

Delegating is different. It requires trusting your employees. You will need to understand your employees' capabilities so you can demonstrate your confidence in them to take on a new project or process and, with some guidance from you, complete the project independently. You must be willing to allow for stumbles and problems as the employees learn new tasks or assume new responsibilities. After all, isn't that how you learned? There is a value added when the project or process is complete and the employee will have a sense of accomplishment. This is how I see delegating. This is what scares the micromanager.

Micromanagers are usually selected as supervisors because they excelled technically. They take pride in that and, because of that, often think no one else can really do the job as well as they can. If they dare to delegate a task to an employee, micromanagers watch very carefully and ask for updates more frequently than expected. They may send frequent nagging emails reminding the employee about the timeline or expectations. The employee quickly regrets taking on the assignment. He senses a lack of trust from the supervisor and that affects motivation to move forward. The final product may suffer – which further "proves" that the micromanager was right not to delegate.

I realize I am picking on MMA-ers but delegation is an essential aspect of effective supervision. It's a skill that will help you get the work done, it serves as a training tool, and it motivates employees to strive to accomplish more than they thought was possible. MMA-ers often forget how *they* learned new skills that helped them to move forward – many were developed from the projects delegated to them on the way up. It's time to pass along the gift.

Why is delegating important?
Helping and delegating will free up valuable time for you. But delegating does more than that – it provides opportunities for your employees.

In addition to freeing up your time, delegating gives the employee a chance to learn a new project, process, technique, and/or responsibility by completing a project independently or perhaps lead a project he or she does well. The employee has a sense of independently earned success. Success breeds pride and accomplishment. When approached carefully, delegating is a win-win. The employee has the satisfaction of bringing value to the unit or work product. Equally important, the supervisor will have the opportunity to focus on top priority projects or issues and, in the process, she gets a more skilled worker.

Effective delegating can be one of your best motivating tools

Effective delegation motivates employees because:

• *It provides opportunity for an employee to learn new skill sets*

• *It provides a sense of accomplishment and contribution to the team work effort*

ॐ

Assess and provide opportunities to learn

When approached carelessly, delegating may damage the relationship between the supervisor and the employee and affect the morale of the team. If an untrained supervisor delegates a project to someone who is not ready to assume additional responsibilities, that employee is doomed to failure. You need to know your employee's skills and abilities before delegating. Review the skills and tasks carefully with the employee so both of you are on the same page before the project begins. Once you've reviewed what skills the employee needs to complete the work, you will also know what kind of training and guidance is necessary. Assume he will need some training. He should know that support is available throughout the entire process.

State the priorities

Another factor that dooms this process is when a supervisor does not provide employee with priorities. Is this new project top priority? Will the supervisor relieve the employee of other tasks to make room for the new project? This needs to be clearly communicated at the start of the project and sometimes renegotiated along the way. I have seen far too many supervisors delegate work to employees without giving prioritization details. The result is a burned out employee, who becomes more prone to making errors or missing deadlines for all projects – routine and the new one. If you don't prioritize tasks together and you wonder why he isn't succeeding, take a look in the mirror.

Offer the opportunity

While I have focused a great deal of the discussion on the problems MMA-ers have with delegation, there are some new supervisors who are afraid to ask someone to do something – "I don't want to seem too bossy, you know?" As if giving employees the opportunity to increase knowledge and participation in the work efforts will hurt their feelings or make them angry. Except in rare instances, this simply isn't true. Effective delegating is actually a very strong motivating tool.

Quick List to Effective Delegating

- *Understand the tasks or responsibilities to delegate*

- *Select the appropriate person*

- *Explain the reason(s) for delegation*

- *Communicate the objectives clearly*

- *Provide training if necessary*

- *Grant authority if necessary*

- *Assign results, not process*

- *Gain commitment*

- *Express positive expectations*

- *Get feedback*

- *Monitor results*

In summary:

- Make sure you know what you want done, that you have the right person to do it, and that the selected employee understands what you want and has the full capacity and tools to complete the project.

- Ask delegated employees if they are willing and able to complete this responsibility and be absolutely certain to get regular feedback.

- Don't wait for employee to struggle. Help her succeed.

- Reward success with positive feedback and appreciation. A total win-win.

Motivating Employees

"How can I motivate my employees?" I get this question from all levels of management – supervisors, managers and executives. Usually, the supervisors and managers have a couple of employees in mind. Executives think in broader terms and want to improve the overall company morale. Motivating others is complex, but there are some concepts and tools that universally work.

What about bonuses?

Monetary bonuses are nice, but some employees only see a bonus as reward for work completed. Bonuses are retroactive. If the bonus is tied to a specific element, such as amount of product completed or increase in sales dollars, the employer can motivate an increase in work production tied to that bonus. However, specific bonuses tied to specific work production are difficult to plan for all employees in a company. While I am a fan of bonus programs tied to corporate and individual goals, such a program requires the implementation of certain and measurable goals, and regular evaluation and monitoring, which is time consuming for management. These programs are usually developed and led by human resources and require staff training to implement properly. They are designed to keep employees focused on the work product and reward for that focus and production. They serve as motivators to some degree, but we need to look at all aspects of motivation.

An overall corporate bonus not tied to individual goals but given to all employees when a company is successful is often graduated by salary level – leaving lower paid employees feeling cynical. While corporate bonuses are nice, they do not have the same motivational impact across salary bands and can sometimes have the opposite effect.

There are some up front bonuses, but they are not intended to improve or increase long-term motivation. A retention bonus, for example, is usually given to a valuable employee who plans to leave the company during a lay off. Sometimes retention bonuses are given when it is important to keep key employees during a company restructure. This is different and not a tool usually available to supervisors.

While everyone likes receiving a bonus, I am not sure that bonuses are the best motivator for individual effort. In some cases, employees come to expect a bonus and the reason for receiving it is lost in the expectation. Some people will stay at a company because of the expectation of the corporate bonus, but that doesn't mean that their individual effort is motivated. Quite the opposite can happen, actually, if an employee stays just because they expect a bonus. Most of the supervisors I speak with are looking for motivating tools that have a long-term positive impact on each employee's desire to do his best.

What **does** motivate an employee?

Employee motivation is internal. Our primary motivation to do well at work is survival – we need work to provide ourselves and our families with food and shelter. We do well so we can keep our job and provide the life basics. Motivation at work is also influenced by other factors such as the type of work we want to do, a sense of fairness, the perceived value of the work, and various social factors. Most of us want to feel good about what we do. We seek to be influenced that way. We want to feel energized, inspired and motivated.

I've conducted many employee surveys to find out what motivates them. The results of the surveys have varied a bit over the years. One commonality is that everyone wants to feel they are being paid a fair wage. Most of us wish for more pay. However, most of us know when we are being paid fairly for our work and in comparison to our peers. Supervisors have very little say in salary scales and pay but if you become aware that there isn't parity among the employee's salaries, it is important to address this issue with your manager and/or human resources. Regardless of your authority in this area, if there is favoritism in pay, you will have a problem with staff motivation. Fair pay is your starting point.

Assuming that salary structures and policy at your company ensure fair pay for all, list three things that motivate you to keep working hard or even improve your work efforts:

1. _____

2. _____

3. _____

I'm betting that many of you listed two or more of the following:

- *Interesting, challenging and/or important work*

- *Professional growth*

- *Appreciation of your work efforts*

- *Positive relationships with fellow employees*

- *Respect from fellow employees*

- *Included in special projects or processes*

- *Positive feedback and recognition from my manager*

This list includes some of the most effective motivating factors found in employee satisfaction surveys. Can you determine what the common denominator is?

Almost every element that plays an important role in employee satisfaction has to do with the employee's positive relationship and communication with supervisors. Look again. Can you see that element in each item on the list?

> *The relationship with the supervisor has the most significant effect on an employee's morale and long-term retention.*

Supervisors have the responsibility of initiating and maintaining communication, offering challenging opportunities and letting those who succeed and excel know that their work is appreciated.

Motivating employees is a day-to-day responsibility for supervisors.

Some specific motivating tools

Here are some suggestions to improve your employees' motivation. Note that each suggestion requires a strong effort on your part:

1. Meet with your employees regularly

    a. Your employees will benefit from knowing that you are interested in them and their concerns.
    b. Ask questions, listen, and make changes that make sense.

2. Meet with your employees immediately if there is a performance issue.

   a. Waiting for performance to improve does not work.
   b. Most employees want to succeed and helping them do so in a positive way lets them know you want them to succeed as well.

3. Help your employee correct deficiencies.

   a. Be pro-active.
   b. Find out what an employee needs to improve and make every effort to provide it.
   c. Follow up and show employees that you continue to want them to succeed.

4. Praise your employee when appropriate.

5. Offer challenging opportunities through a delegation program.

   a. Opportunities to grow professionally in a way that can lead to increases in responsibility, improved job title and greater pay are highly motivating factors to most employees.

6. Respect all employees regardless of their performance.

7. Have a little fun. Make it a good day for others.

Playing favorites

One of the most frustrating employee problems I had as a human resource director was caused by a scientific director, Steve, who clearly had a blind spot when it came to assessing the value of one of his assistants, Marianne. Marianne was the project coordinator for Steve's unit. Steve had known Marianne for many years and had worked with her at another company. He hired her shortly after he arrived at our firm and immediately put her to work managing projects in his department. With Marianne in place, Steve made little effort to get to know his staff. Marianne was his conduit. Time frames for completing projects were set by Marianne regardless of input from staff scientists, and Marianne's critical comments about the work efforts of his staff were accepted unequivocally by Steve. He rarely met with any other team member.

Frustrated employees in Steve's team were regular visitors to my office. After hearing the stories, all of which spoke of favoritism, I went down the hall to visit with Steve. My attempts to broaden his perspective were met with stony expressions and suggestions that I mind my own business. I maintained an open dialogue with Steve, expecting that, in no time, the morale of his group would begin to suffer and he would need some help. I was hoping he would come to me. He did.

Eventually, Steve was willing to accept the fact that he had made a serious mistake by limiting his interactions with his staff and accepting the information and perspective of only one employee. He began to realize that, while trusting Marianne, someone he all ready

124

knew, was understandable, his singular focus probably cost him the benefits of his talented and enthusiastic team. In fact, Steve's focus on just one employee also cost him the trust of his staff. They became wary and silent around Marianne and rarely spoke with Steve. Unfortunately, at this point it was impossible to turn things around completely with the staff he had. In time, because of turnover and a more prudent approach to all of his new team, the morale and productivity of his team did improve.

We've all had a sense at one time or another that "so-and-so likes her best." It's an uncomfortable feeling because regardless of who we are or how we do something, it's a foregone conclusion that someone else will get the goodies just because she is "liked best." At some level, this is part of the human experience. Remember the teacher's pet? In the end we didn't like the teacher and we weren't too fond of her pet, either.

When speaking of a "favorite employee," I am not referring to the top performer who helps every day to make your group successful. I am not referring to the employee who makes your job easier by helping others or taking initiative that helps the company improve. These are employees you can count on. They have been tested with time. Their accomplishments are also evident to other employees on the team, but those team members do not sense that you have excluded their talents to the benefit of your top performer. The reality is that top performers are probably the future supervisors and leaders of your group and your staff knows that.

Developing an employee's desire to work hard and well is easier when it is clear to the employee that his work effort is valued and appreciated.

∾

Supervising Former Peers

It's tough going from peer to supervisor for a number of reasons:

- *You may not have been trained to supervise.*

- *Your peers may be jealous.*

- *You want to continue to be friends with your peers.*

- *Some of your former peers may expect your relationship to stay the same.*

- *You are a bit scared about all of this or you are overconfident. Neither state of mind is helpful.*

It's not typical, but I have seen some people transition from peer to supervisor with considerable ease. One fellow, Tom, didn't seem fazed with his new supervisory responsibilities at all. The men (yes, all men) in his unit automatically accepted his new leadership role. I like to watch change and how people manage it. Going from peer to supervisor is a big transition, so Tom's ability to successful manage his new role was particularly interesting. Here are some observations that may help you.

Tom was good at his work. He had a reputation of being strong in his area of expertise. He was a hard worker who applied his knowledge well and he was respected.

He shared his knowledge with others and was quick to acknowledge his peers' successes. Tom's confidence in his own professional skills seemed to reduce the need to take credit for or diminish the success of others.

Tom treated everyone with respect. He seemed comfortable and enjoyed working with his peers. It seemed like he was offering assistance rather than criticism when someone struggled. He was that way before his promotion and continued to be that way afterward. His reputation as someone you could go to for help was strongly imprinted on his peers. His knack for making others look good continued as a supervisor.

Prior to his promotion, Tom had willingly accepted an assignment as a trainer. This was a valuable experience and reinforced a number of supervisory concepts after his promotion.

I chatted with Tom at times and was pleasantly surprised to learn that he was pretty firm about valuing respect more than likability. "As much as I like being liked," he said, "being treated with respect is a higher priority for me. Respect means they understand what is expected and accept that without qualification. I can't make them respect me; I have to earn their respect. I do this by knowing my trade, working hard, setting a good example and helping my staff succeed. It's not easy, but it does pay off."

"What about my friends?" This is the conundrum. You got promoted and your best friend didn't. Yikes. If you are following the concepts of this book, you know that being a supervisor doesn't mean you suddenly you become Atilla the Hun. You and your friend might need a bit of chat. You can't control how other people will feel. You *can* control your own actions. Applying the concepts that Tom used will go a long way toward reassuring your friends that you are the kind of supervisor who is interested in everyone's success. It's likely that others in the group are aware of your friendship. Watch for that favorites-thing because you will need everyone on your team to make it all work.

If you didn't come to this new job as well-prepared as you would have liked, the challenge might seem overwhelming. Talk to a more experienced manager or a human resource professional. Most of these managers have been in your shoes. Share the concepts in this chapter with your manager and find ways to apply the information specifically to your work situation and the people on your team. Remember – change requires time and patience.

Tom's Tips

- Know your technical work

- Set an example

- Help others succeed

- Share the glory

- Respect others

- Being liked is nice; being respected is essential

NOTES:

Meeting Management

I remember my first senior management meeting when I worked for an international firm. I had been attending meetings at various organizations and had certain meeting format expectations. This meeting was set once a month at 10:00 a.m. As a newcomer and someone who liked to watch meeting participants, I wanted a decent seat in this large room and arrived about five minutes early. Not a soul was there. Some employees came straggling in around 10:00, when strangely there were still lots of seats available. By 10:15 it seemed everyone had arrived except the president of the company who was the facilitator. No one was concerned. As an adult who likely has a mild case of undiagnosed ADHD, I'm wiggling in my chair. I thought we'd be through a couple of agenda items by now. Its 10:30 and we were finally good to go. Well, except there was no agenda. Everyone was calm except me. Looking back, everyone actually seemed disengaged and that was also becoming true for me. The topics shifted without direction and some participants rambled along taking the lion's share of time. Some participants pulled out their PDAs and drifted through their emails as though they were alone in the room. The meeting droned on and on.

Sound familiar?

132

Turns out the attendees at this meeting were among the 85 percent of employees who think meetings are a waste of time where nothing gets accomplished. They had the experience to prove it.

It's not the meetings that are the problem. It's the facilitators. Well-run meetings can actually save time, improve communication and facilitate work. Unfortunately, most supervisors and managers don't know how to run a meeting.

Most people love to hear themselves talk. Some like to dominate group discussions. Ever notice that there is usually one really good rambling talker in every meeting? We all have. Sometimes it's also the rambling talker who is often the most likely to complain that people talk too much in meetings. I had one of those talkers as a client. He went on and on about people who talk too much. He blathered endlessly about how to control such behavior. I had a sense that running effective meetings would not be his strong suit.

Frankly, if you are not prepared, running a meeting is like herding cats. It's not easy, but it can be done with the right tools. Let's get prepared.

Essential Elements to Meeting Management

The basic premise of a well-run meeting is respecting your participants. Respect their time, expertise and desire to participate productively in a team. Each of these meeting essentials conveys respect for the participants:

1. Have a clearly defined <u>purpose</u> for each meeting.

2. Invite the <u>fewest number of people and only those who absolutely need to be there</u> in order to accomplish the purpose of the meeting.

3. Have an <u>agenda</u> for every meeting.

   ↪ List points of discussion in order

   ↪ Distribute the agenda in advance

   ↪ Encourage employees to be prepared for the meeting

4. Agree on basic <u>rules</u> for the meeting.

   ↪ For example:

      ▪ Begin on time and end on time. Respect everyone's time.

      ▪ Set a time limit and stick to it. Most meetings can be done in 30 to 60 minutes. After 60 minutes, most employees lose focus and energy.

- Respect everyone's opinion. This is where you can clarify what "talking too long" is for this meeting. You can also forewarn participants that, if necessary, you as the facilitator reserve the right to re-direct the conversation to another attendee.

- Keep comments brief. Many people like to hear themselves talk. It is the facilitator's responsibility to minimize this tendency.

5. Have <u>action items</u>. Distribute these to the attendees after the meeting.

6. <u>Follow through</u> on previous action items and accountabilities. Perhaps you can make this the first agenda topic for each meeting.

Let's talk about some of the problem areas here. Many companies have meetings because it's a "time for us to connect." May I suggest pizza at lunch or bagels in the morning for connecting with your employees?

At one company, my boss thought it was a good idea to have a weekly meeting so everyone could share what we had accomplished the prior week. Everyone began trying to remember what they had accomplished during that timeframe. We all wanted to sound busy and productive. The focus of the meeting had nothing to do with future planning or employee concerns. It became the "dreaded Monday morning brag meeting."

Meetings are intended to relate to the business of the

group. If you can't name a purpose, it's probably not a good idea to have the meeting. Your ability to clearly state the purpose of the meeting tells the participants what you hope to accomplish. This gives everyone a focus.

Having an agenda is a problem for many supervisors. They tell me that they "don't have the time" or that, "Everyone knows what's up." However, when employees aren't really sure what the meeting is about, they are not prepared for discussion. It is not surprising when no one says anything at a meeting where there's no agenda. If you come to your meetings unprepared, no one knows what to expect. Under those circumstances, who wants to go first? Not me.

Employees should know what you expect from them. Set some rules. One of the most important rules is that meetings start on time. I once had a manager who, when facilitating a meeting, would abruptly stop speaking and quietly watch each latecomer enter the room. Embarrassment can be an effective change agent, though it's not my favorite. The meeting attendees deserve to have their time respected. If you come late, so will they.

Start on time and end on time.

Action items. A good reason to have a meeting is to plan to get work done. How many meetings have you attended where the facilitator delegates a project only to have it disappear into a black hole? It happens all the time.

Here's an idea:

𝕿 Either you or someone you ask takes notes of the action items that require follow up. Keep those notes to track the action items and append an update to subsequent meetings until the conclusion has been reached.

"Work Sessions"

This term came up during a training session on effective meetings where I had some push back regarding agendas and planning for work projects. Many companies have a creative group which needs to meet occasionally to encourage creative juices to flow. Some rambling can be helpful in these sessions. To distinguish these meetings from the more formal agenda-driven meetings, I suggested they call these creative gatherings "work sessions." There's a purpose and hopefully some ideas at the end, but these sessions are informal and imaginative.

If this idea works for you, make the distinction. Just make sure your attendees know what to expect before they go to the sessions.

Individual Meetings

I have made quite a few references to meeting individually with your employees. Here's some guidance to that may help make these meetings meaningful and effective.

Think about the logistics. Ever been to the Big Boss' office? Big Room, Big Chair, Big, Big, Big. You get to sit precisely three feet on the other side of that Big Desk and tell Big Boss what's on your mind. Doesn't feel so good, does it? If you have an office, look around. How is it set up? Got that guest chair on the other side of your desk? Do you have that monitor positioned so you can glance down in case a *very* important email comes in? Maybe your chair sits at an angle. Look around and decide if this is inviting. If it's not, change it so there is a sense of connection when someone enters.

I have been pretty lucky with my office size because of the type of work I do. I've usually had a work table that is separate from my desk. When an employee comes in, I get up from behind my desk and go to the table. I sit across from another chair and ask the employee to join me. This removes the physical barriers between us and invites the person into a conversation. The employee knows I am welcoming him to my office, he has my full attention and I am ready to engage. If you don't have that work table, consider having a chair on the *side* of your desk for meetings with individuals. Take away that barrier.

If you are in a cubicle, it is impossible to provide the same type of accommodation. However, you can ask the employee if the meeting requires privacy. If it does, make every effort to find a private space and arrange yourself in such a fashion that the employee knows you are ready to meet.

If the meeting is quick and informational, you should still make some accommodations to let your employees know you're fully there. All of your employees deserve this. Look up and acknowledge your employee. If you are not able to meet at that moment, just say so. This is much better than your employee finding herself talking to the side of your head and hoping you respond.

Let's assume the individual meeting is meant to be private and is important to you or the employee. After establishing a welcome, it is your responsibility to open the conversation.

Opening remarks:

↬ *How can I help you?*

↬ *I want to talk to you about...*

Simple phrases, but opening a dialogue doesn't require more.

During the meeting:

↬ *So what I hear you saying is ...*

↬ *Can you help me understand what happened in this situation?*

Ensure that, when the meeting has ended, you and the employee both understand what has been said.

At the end:

- ⊷ *Let's meet next Tuesday at the same time to talk about the progress.*

- ⊷ *So what you'd like me to do is…*

- ⊷ *Can I have your commitment to improving in…?*

These types of comments summarize and confirm the agreed upon action items.

The basic tenets of an individual meeting follow those of the group meeting. This meeting forum is just more personal.

A well-run meeting shows respect for your employees.

- *Don't have a meeting if you don't need one.*

- *Know when you need to have a meeting and do it.*

- *Meetings can be very short. They shouldn't be too long.*

- *Know why you are having a meeting and be sure those who attend know why you are having the meeting.*

- *Have a purpose and an agenda.*

- *Know how to plan for your meetings.*

- *Know how to control your meetings.*

- *Follow up on action items.*

Here is a survey form for your meeting group. Try it. The results may be helpful as you assess the effectiveness of your meeting management.

MEETING SURVEY FORM

1= Fully Agree
5 = Do not agree at all

1.	We used everyone as a resource	1	2	3	4	5
2.	We used our time effectively	1	2	3	4	5
3.	We stayed focused on our tasks	1	2	3	4	5
4.	We listened to each other	1	2	3	4	5
5.	We resolved differences positively and respectfully	1	2	3	4	5
6.	We accomplished our meeting objectives	1	2	3	4	5
7.	We followed through on our actoin items	1	2	3	4	5

Suggestions for improvement:

NOTES:

The New Employee

Sadly, many employees do not have the best day on their first day at work. It's pretty easy to blame human resources. Maybe you work for a company where the new employee program is boring, confusing, detached or (worse) absent. This will not be a good start for the enthusiastic new employee. However, because you will be *the most important person* to the new employee, his experience with you will have the biggest impact.

One of my clients, Sam, supervised about fifteen help desk technicians. Sam's day was filled with putting out fires – like customer computer issues, or fielding complaints about the help desk technicians who couldn't solve those problems. When I met Sam, he was overwhelmed with repair work and people problems. Most of the time, he was angry that his techs weren't performing despite the fact they were all well-credentialed. Sam had no prior experience supervising employees, and was promoted because he was an excellent technician. Sound familiar? Sam hadn't been trained as a new supervisor so he spent his days winging it. It was not a pretty picture – his employees received inconsistent interaction and Sam felt that he was in constant crisis mode.

Sam was discouraged. His staff did not seem cohesive,

144

there was high absenteeism and work was not completed in a timely fashion. Overall, he was unhappy with his employees and their performance. He was at a loss.

We started with the basics – how were new employees welcomed and trained? "By human resources," he said. Once a new employee came to his unit, he figured they were ready to learn the IT systems at the company. Each new employee was given a week to train on the system and were then told to, "Feel free to ask questions whenever they wanted." End of training.

We began the new program by reviewing how each employee had joined the company, how much time Sam had spent with them, what he knew about them, how each one fit into the group and what their career goals were. He was astonished to find how little information he had about his employees. He didn't know much besides their names and assignments. Both of us agreed that some changes needed to be made. Sam was an active participant as we developed the New Employee Plan for his unit. This may be helpful to you, as well.

The New Employee Plan:

1. Sam will personally <u>welcome each new employee</u>. He will accompany each one to his/her well-stocked workstation. Each new employee will be introduced to the other team members.

2. Sam will <u>arrange a one-on-one meeting on the employee's first day</u>. One purpose of the meeting is to learn about the employee as a person. Sam will share a bit about himself, too. Sam will also discuss the purpose of the unit and how it fits into the needs of the company. He will talk about how his group works and what his general expectations are for the group as a whole. The meeting will take no longer than an hour, but preferably thirty minutes. If more than one employee arrives on a given day, he can meet with both at the same time.

3. Sam will <u>arrange for the new employee to have a "Transition Mentor."</u> This mentor, a peer but not necessarily a technician, will show the new employee how to get supplies, explain various meetings, tell him who does what from a staffer's point of view, and give information on how to get around town if the employee is new to the area. The company will pay for one lunch if that is mutually acceptable to the new employee and mentor. The Transition Mentor is a company companion or advocate during the orientation period for up to two weeks. The Transition Mentor goes to the new employee, rather than have the new employee seek out someone for general assistance.

4. Sam developed a thorough help desk <u>training program,</u> and assigned a designated trainer to work with new employees on technical training. The trainer is assigned for up to one month and advises Sam if the new employee seems to be struggling. In that case, Sam meets with the new employee to evaluate the best way to help. Assigning an employee to be a "trainer" for new employees can be an effective motivation tool. It can also provide an opportunity for the employee to develop some leadership skills.

5. Finally, Sam will <u>follow-up with the new employee at the end of the three-month probationary period</u>. If the employee has successfully completed the probationary period, together they will review the new employee's progress and identify any concerns or outstanding issues. If there *are* any outstanding issues, Sam and the new employee commit to working these out.

Within three months, after implementing this orientation program with five new employees, as well as some of the veteran employees, the group's mood was clearly shifting. Employees were interacting very well on an informal basis and helping each other when the work load got heavy. Over a six-month period, turn-over decreased. Much of Sam's chaotic day was improved.

Welcome your new employee:

- ➤ *Get to know him*

- ➤ *Assign a co-worker to serve as a transition mentor*

- ➤ *Train him*

- ➤ *Follow up to determine the success of the training and any outstanding issue*

❧

Managing Up

"Managing up" is an important tool for any employee who wants to succeed professionally. It is an *essential* tool for an effective supervisor. If you think that your manager is blocking your progress or making things difficult, you are probably not managing up. If you learn this skill you and your employees will have a greater chance of getting what you need to succeed.

So, what is managing up?

> *Managing up is increasing the likelihood that your manager will work productively with you to meet the needs of your unit and employees.*

When a new supervisor complains to me that he is not getting support from his manager, I ask what he thinks is going on. Often the supervisor sees himself as a victim of some strange decision tree. He says he's waiting for his manager to approve this or that, and he begins to criticize the manager. You know "My manager did this, my manager is so unfair, my director just implements programs without understanding the impact on my team." The complaints about managers are endless and take many productive work hours out of the day. Who doesn't complain, really?

If your manager is implementing inefficient programs, faulty processes, or "making a mess of things," have you looked at how you may be contributing? Have you thought that maybe you can help your supervisor improve? Have you tried to manage up?

You might say, "Well, my supervisor never listens to me anyway. She just does what she wants." I have heard that line many times. While there are some managers who resist suggestions or discussion, that isn't always (or even mostly) true. You won't get everything you want when you manage up, but in most cases you will get some change. Be realistic in your expectation for change because if you approach this process with a positive attitude and careful planning, you will see change for the better. Most of us change in small ways and take small steps. This is probably true for you as you grow in your supervisory skills. It will be true for your manager as she learns to ask questions, listen, and discuss the situation to determine what you need to succeed.

Some supervisors that I coach are quite skeptical of this concept and accuse me of wanting them to "brown-nose." I worked with a senior scientist, Mel, several years ago. He was excellent at the technical part of his job and supervised four bench level associates. They were a good team and had recently completed a major project that helped seal a pharmaceutical deal worth quite a bit of money. The problem for Mel was that his group was low on the totem pole for budget allocations. The group never seemed to get the public kudos he thought they deserved. They worked hard and Mel thought they deserved some kind of acknowledgement at the very least.

I agreed with him and invited him to lunch.

I asked him how often he met with his director, Sue. "Maybe once a month." "How do you update Sue?" I asked. "Emails," was Mel's reply. "How about budget allocations? Did you work with Sue on that?" He said, "No, I get the budget numbers once a year and that's it. I never get asked for my opinion. I doubt she really cares." It became clear that Mel was not an active participant in the management process. Other project leaders, who were more proactive in managing up, were getting the goodies. Mel had a reputation of being easygoing but I saw a passive manager.

When I began making suggestions to Mel, he became defensive immediately. As a reply to my suggestion that maybe he go to lunch with the manager and open a dialogue for future meetings, he said he wasn't a "brown-noser." I encouraged him to network with his company peers. "Have coffee, find out how things are working for them, what challenges they have, etc." Mel said, "I don't want to push myself on them."

Mel may be an extreme example of passive management, but it is a common affliction with new supervisors to some degree.

Tips to Managing Up

These tools can help you manage up:

Get to know your manager.

- 🦚 How does she work with her employees? What is important to her at work? What are her strengths and challenges as you see them? How does she work best? Who does she work best with? What is her work style? How does she receive information best (written, verbal)? What does she dislike?

- 🦚 Watch her in meetings. How does she interact with others and how does she manage the group and the work assignments? Observe, observe, observe.

Take the initiative to meet with your manager regularly and make the meetings count.

- 🦚 Your meetings count if you go in with information that will help your manager best receive it, process it, and discuss it. Remember, you are trying to get your manager to see your point of view. **Present it so he gets it.**

- 🦚 Your meetings will be effective if you **have an agenda and topics prepared**. This can simply be informal notes or, if he seems to do better with a heads up, send a pre-meeting email outlining what you want to talk about.

- **Be succinct**. I like to talk, but I learned quickly that most managers do not want to spend a long time hearing all the extenuating circumstances and anything else you want to get off your chest. Get to the meat quickly.

- **Know what you want to gain from the meeting**. You need to go to your meeting with specific objectives in mind. Articulate them clearly and provide information supporting your request. Are you looking for more money to buy a piece of equipment or an increase in staff? It's not a good idea to just go in and ask for more staff and expect that to happen. Why do you need more staff? Where are the holes in the work effort? What are you doing to fill those holes? Can your manager see other ways to help with this problem?

- **Come prepared with solutions**. Managers hear about problems all day. If you bring some solutions for discussion, you move the discussion forward and gain your manager's respect at the same time.

- A favorite phrase of mine is: "**I need some guidance from you**." I do. How else will I get to know what my manager wants if I don't ask for guidance – another way to put this is, "How do you see this happening?" I prefer asking for guidance, but find your own phrase that lets him know you care about what he wants. Many of the supervisors I coach think there is a weakness in asking for help. That's not so. Don't you like to be asked for guidance or help sometimes? You don't need help every day but you can use some help or guidance on certain issues. Seek this from your manager. These should be interactive discussions. You present the problem or issue, ask questions, provide some solutions, and ask for guidance. Come on, let's talk.

Be prepared to lobby for your group.

   ℮ Have the issue researched, present facts, include options, ask for opinions and then ask for what your group needs. If you have done your homework and pay attention to how your manager is responding, then your efforts will more likely pay off. Be flexible and ready for a challenge. This isn't personal. It is essential for making sure the manager has explored the issue well and has all the facts necessary to make the decision.

My last manager did not like lengthy discussions. He liked to be prepared for the meeting, he liked facts, and he always liked to think about the information before making a final decision. For an impatient person like me, that wait was difficult. I often had to return and remind my manager of our conversation. It's not that he didn't care, though one could think that way. He was just overwhelmed with a heavy workload. It was my job to bring the needs of my unit back to his radar. Blaming him for taking too long didn't get me anywhere. Reminding him without nagging usually worked.

<u>You do not need to like your manager to manage up.</u>

We all have natural chemistry with certain people. We all respond negatively, for a variety of reasons, to some people. That's life. It helps to like your manager, but your goal is to effectively supervise your group. That requires you to work cooperatively with your manager. Maybe you do more giving than receiving in the cooperative part of that sentence. So be it. Your job is to help your employees get *their* job done. Manage up whether it is easy or not. In time you may actually find more to like in your manager than you first realized. If not, you are still doing your job as a supervisor.

Thank your manager

It's nice to get a thank you once in a while, isn't it? If your manager is responding to you, and helping you and your group, she deserves a thank you. Don't forget it.

I know there are some of you reading this that are thinking, "Thank her for what?" You don't have to wait for something big to happen, something tangible to notice, or for some kind of gift before you offer thanks. A thank you can be, and often is best, for simple things. Here are some acknowledgements that we all like to hear:

- *Thank you for listening.*

- *I sure appreciate your guidance.*

- *Your support really helped me.*

- *I appreciate your time.*

- *Great idea (even if you initially thought of it).*

- *Thanks for stopping by.*

Everybody likes to be thanked. Give it freely and there will be great rewards for this simple gesture.

- > Get to know your manager

- > Your manager needs information to do the job. Take the initiative to provide it.

- > Your manager should know what you need. Tell him in a way that he best receives it.

- > Your manager wants to be kept updated on progress. Let him know how things are going.

∽

Leadership

It's been said that leaders are born, not made. There may be some truth to that, but people can learn to be leaders. There are innate qualities, such as charisma, evident in some leaders but having that quality alone does not guarantee a good leader. Charisma is also evident in many successful actors. However, few actors are leaders. People want to follow charismatic individuals. Charisma is a gift, not a skill. <u>Effective</u> leadership is more valuable and <u>it can be learned</u>. Solid leadership has a more profound, long-term effect. People will follow true leadership even when the leader is not present.

Many new supervisors become uncomfortable when we begin to discuss leadership. They think leadership is for "someone else." Not so. There is no reason why *you* can't be a strong leader. A supervisor is the leader of a small group of employees. Developing leadership skills is essential if you want to be a strong supervisor. There are many aspects to leadership but, for the new supervisor, let's focus on five of the most basic elements. This is the "Fab Five of Leadership."

The Fab Five of Leadership

1. Set a good example

Setting a good example lays the groundwork for leadership. Like it or not, your staff will judge your integrity, your work ethic, and your work quality. It's very difficult to look up to and want to follow someone who does not have the highest standards. Set an example of professionalism, too. Grouchy, picky, highly emotional, sneaky and unpredictable people can aspire to lead but they won't. They can get the job title but they won't be respectable leaders. Leaders know that people respond to positive energy. True leaders care and those who work with them know that. Leaders emit positive energy and keep a level head when a crisis happens. Strive to set that example and you will be on the path to leadership. You can do this on your first day at work. Continue to set a good example throughout your professional life.

2. Be an effective communicator

Being an effective communicator isn't easy. I've devoted many pages to communication because, as a supervisor and leader, it is your most important tool.

Here are a few more thoughts regarding communication that are well suited to this topic:

- ✓ When communicating with co-workers, remember **to keep your message consistent**. You will do this naturally if you have strong core beliefs and values that do not shift. Don't say what you think someone else wants to hear just so you seem agreeable. This doesn't mean you can forget your communication manners and the value of diplomacy. An open, flexible mind is important, too. However, if you want your staff to come to work on time – a basic rule in the workplace that you have set – don't suddenly change your mind because a staff member you favor can't do that. Your employees need to know they can count on you to have consistent values and attitudes.

✓ **Keeping your language calm and deliberative** during intense discussions or disagreements isn't easy. Composure under pressure is a skill we often need to develop. It is easy to get caught up in the moment or to get angry with a very difficult or disrespectful employee. When things get heated, slow down or pause. If you are upset, it's best to end the meeting and resume talking later when you are calm and composed. If you let your emotions dominate your communication, your ability to help others work through problems diminishes greatly. You become one of the group and certainly not the leader.

✓ Finally, begin to **focus on your ability to persuade**. For some, this may take some time but all top leaders share that quality. This doesn't mean you have to change everyone's mind to think like yours. Persuading others includes finding common ground.

***Effective persuasion means that everyone is
satisfied to some degree.***

The art of persuasion is a study in itself, but there are some basic elements that can help:

> *First – here I go again – listen. How can you alter someone's ideas if you don't know what they are?*

> *Have your facts true and clear. If you are chewing around the edges of the truth just to "get your own way," it won't hold up in the long run.*

> *Offer various solutions. Solicit the same from the person or persons you are trying to persuade.*

> *Listen again.*

> *Wrap it up. Review the agreed upon solutions, offer and be prepared to make the solutions work.*

> *Finally, show gratitude to someone working with you.*

Give this a try and you'll be getting your way more often.

3. Focus on results

No one wants to follow a person who can't get things done. Your job as a leader is to keep things under control and moving forward – not micromanage the work. Set a clear purpose. The group you are leading needs to know what the purpose is, feel confident that it can get done, and that you will help with that endeavor. If they don't know what you want, they won't know where you

Made in the USA
Lexington, KY
08 November 2015

are going.

4.   Enthusiasm and Energy

I am not talking about being the happy cheerleader here. Simply be a person that other people like being around. If you complain about management, the company, the product, process, peers or your staff, you are not a leader. A leader works to improve problems. Leaders do not drop those problems on others. I have worked with some new supervisors who like to be a part of the grapevine. This isn't good. Leaders don't participate in gossip. This may not be easy but, if you are seen as part of the gossip club, you won't be the best leader you can be.

Most people respond positively to the energy of others. You get to chose – Sour-puss Suzie or Engaging Emily. Which one would you want to spend time with? Employers can sense when someone positively supports fellow employees and the company's work product. They are more likely to reward the employee with a positive attitude than one who is detached and grouchy. As a supervisor, your staff will more likely reward you with loyalty and hard work if you give them a sense that you like working with them and support the company.

5.   Bring out the best in others

This is my favorite. It requires confidence in yourself. It demands the desire to help other people succeed. It is a subtle skill to acquire, but it's invaluable. If you can get people to believe in themselves more than they do, their desire to develop and to work hard for you is limitless. Think of that special teacher you had in school. We usu-

ally remember his or her name and the subject matter or special stories we shared. We probably learned that subject better than we expected to. For some people, such a teacher impacted our life's work.

I had a manager like this as I was developing my career. I'll always think of him as a teacher. His name was John and he was the president of a small biotechnology company. He was one of those charismatic individuals who made the day a bit brighter. He had boundless energy. Everyone liked being around him, including me. John was highly respected by everyone for his business abilities. I was the human resource and administrative manager. We were a small company, so most of us wore many hats. My nature is geared more toward language than math or science. Honestly, I couldn't balance my checkbook without a calculator if my life depended on it. I have other skills, though, and when problems arose in the finance department, John figured some of those skills could go a long way. I objected vehemently. "John, I can hardly add," I said.

"I don't need you to add. I need you to see what some of the staff *isn't* adding. I need you to find the holes, where the checks are going, and what the heck is going on over there. I need you to figure out why the balance sheet isn't balanced." He taught me how to read a balance sheet. He reviewed the various roles in finance, all of which were pretty junior because of the size of the company. Then he sent me off to figure out what we needed in that department. I was terrified.

John's plan to send in someone like me, who needed to learn about the financial systems, helped the finance

types by forcing them to teach me the systems and tell me how things were getting done. We all began to work together. The finance-types had the numbers and I was organizing, communicating and coordinating. We all began to learn from each other. I could track, make charts, gather missing information and help the group communicate better and coordinate their efforts. After a while, the group found ways to improve the checks and balances. The balance sheets were balancing and pride emerged from this small group. It didn't take a financial genius to do this. It took someone whose manager said she could learn the basics and offer her complementary skills. John's confidence in my supervisory skills along with my desire to learn and to help others get the job done helped this small group get the job done. I was so proud of myself. Thanks, John, for the vote of confidence. You always made me feel I was smarter and more capable than I thought I was. However, I still don't like working with numbers.

Leadership's Fab Five:

> *Set a good example*

> *Be an effective communicator*

> *Focus on results*

> *Enthusiasm and energy*

> *Bring out the best in others*

NOTES:

Final Thoughts...

Supervision is a moving target. After all, we are dealing with people and there are no absolutes when it comes to human behavior. However, I hope this book provides some perspective relevant to your challenges as a supervisor and practical guidelines that you can try.

I also hope to let you know that you are not alone as you develop supervision skills. As long as we have work units or groups of people trying to get something accomplished, there will be supervisors, coordinators, managers or leaders. Regardless of the title or place, the experiences and need for solutions will be similar. It's good to know this whether you are in the learning phase of your new supervisory role or even if you have grappled with supervision for years. Maybe this book can serve as a point of discussion for you and your peers.

I want to emphasize one last thing. There are many fine books and articles on supervising people. Most of us write so we can share our experiences, our knowledge and offer solutions. One thing is certain, though. No one has all the answers when it comes to people management. You may try "this" or "that" and still be frustrated with your efforts to effect change. Sometimes, with fellow humans, we just get stuck. I hope that I have offered you some flexibility in your thinking. If I have, progress is happening.

The most flexible and important advice I offer you is in the question you can ask your employees. "*How can I help?*" And then, of course, please listen.

❧

Acknowledgements

I would like to express my deepest gratitude to the many people who saw me through this book.

First thanks to Sherri Bale for suggesting I share my knowledge and write a book about supervising employees. What a wonderful and challenging experience this has been for me. Thanks, Sherri, for getting me started.

Many thanks to friends and family, who listened endlessly to me blather about this or that part of the book. Thanks go out to those of you who read bits and pieces of forming chapters when I started this project. I needed some kind of acknowledgement and encouragement that I could do this, and you gave it to me when there wasn't much evidence that I could actually write. You believed in me and that was wonderful. Thanks to those of you who actually read and helped edit the final draft and the final-final draft and then the very last final draft with apparent interest. You were very good at making me feel like each read was the first. Thanks to all of you – Sherri Bale, Bryn 'Taffy' Weymouth, Marge Meyer, Lorraine Blackman, Isabelle Olivos-Glander, Tina D'Souza, and my lovely and intelligent daughter, Rachel Hugg.

I had wonderful, steady professional editors. Thanks to Jessica Tyner, who helped me write less and say more, and to Genna Marie Robustelli who guided me through

the formatting and graphic design. She did a spectacular job with a delightful sense of enthusiasm.

Finally, my hubby, my best friend, my cheerleader and
all-around enthusiast, Richard – the biggest hug and
thanks for your guidance and steady confidence.